A Primer on Crime and Delinquency Theory

Second Edition

ROBERT M. BOHM
University of Central Florida

WADSWORTH
—————★————— TM
THOMSON LEARNING

Australia • Canada • Mexico • Singapore • Spain
United Kingdom • United States

WADSWORTH

THOMSON LEARNING™

Criminal Justice Editor: *Sabra Horne*
Development Editor: *Terri Edwards*
Assistant Editor: *Ann Tsai*
Editorial Assistant: *Cortney Bruggink*
Marketing Manager: *Jennifer Somerville*
Marketing Assistant: *Karyl Davis*
Project Editor: *Dianne Jensis Toop*
Print Buyer: *Robert King*

Permissions Editor: *Joohee Lee*
Production Service: *Gustafson Graphics*
Copy Editor: *Linda Ireland*
Cover Designer: *Yvo Riezebos*
Cover Printer: *Webcom Limited*
Compositor: *Gustafson Graphics*
Printer: *Webcom Limited*

Printed in Canada
2 3 4 5 6 7 03 02 01

For permission to use material from this text, contact
us: **Web:** http://www.thomsonrights.com
Fax: 1-800-730-2215 **Phone:** 1-800-730-2214

For more information, contact
Wadsworth/Thomson Learning
10 Davis Drive
Belmont, CA 94002-3098
USA
http://www.wadsworth.com

International Headquarters
Thomson Learning
International Division
290 Harbor Drive, 2nd Floor
Stamford, CT 06902-7477
USA

UK/Europe/Middle East/South Africa
Thomson Learning
Berkshire House
168-173 High Holborn
London WC1V 7AA
United Kingdom

Asia
Thomson Learning
60 Albert Street, #15-01
Albert Complex
Singapore 189969

Canada
Nelson Thomson Learning
1120 Birchmount Road
Toronto, Ontario M1K 5G4
Canada

Library of Congress Cataloging-in-Publication Data

Bohm, Robert M.
    A primer on crime and delinquency theory / Robert M. Bohm.—2nd ed.
        p. cm.
    Rev. ed. of: A primer on crime and delinquency. c1997.
    Includes bibliographical references and index.
    ISBN 0-534-54158-5
        1. Criminology. 2. Crime. I. Bohm, Robert M. Primer on crime and
    delinquency. II. Title.
HV6018 .B645 2000
364—dc21   00-043762

Dedicated to
my Mom and Dad,
Elizabeth and Jack Bohm

Contents

Preface

My primary purpose in writing this book was to provide both undergraduate and graduate students with a relatively brief but comprehensive exposition of crime and delinquency theories. The book should prove useful either as a primary text (with instructor supplements) or as a supplement to other texts, anthologies, or collections of journal articles.

Although many fine criminological texts are on the market, none of them provides precisely the material or the material in a manner that I believe students of crime and delinquency theory ought to receive. For example, some texts contain much more material than ever can be covered satisfactorily within the time constraints of an academic semester or quarter. Consequently, instructors are forced to ignore some theories or offer a superficial rendering of some of the theories that they do present. With this slim volume, instructors need not worry about such time constraints but still can be confident that they are presenting a reasonably comprehensive description. Some texts focus only on one or another theoretical perspective and thus ignore the rich multidisciplinary nature of crime and delinquency theory. For example, many criminological texts present only sociological theories, or, when other theories are examined, they are given short shrift. This text, though brief, is comprehensive and multidisciplinary in its scope.

Few of the available criminological texts provide what I consider an adequate introduction to theory. For example, conspicuously missing from most texts are discussions of the critically important issues of the philosophical assumptions on which all theories are based and how theories can be judged in relation to each other. I hope that this book rectifies each of those omissions. Also, although other texts present descriptions of the theories, few of them identify the policy implications that are either explicit or implicit in all theories. A major feature of this book is the description of the policy implications of the theories. Perhaps most importantly, very few of the available texts incorporate a comprehensive critique of the theories. Again, a principal feature of this book is a thorough critique of each of the theories.

In an effort to keep this book "a primer," I needed to exclude many of the theorists who have contributed to the development of various crime and delinquency theories. My hope is that students will augment the theoretical formulations presented in this book by examining the works (in books and journal articles) of other theorists. Indeed, a useful exercise for students would be to trace the development of a theory from its initial formulation through its most recent developments.

In sum, the first edition, *A Primer on Crime and Delinquency,* provided in a very manageable format (1) an introduction to theory with a special focus on the philosophical assumptions of theories and how the theories can be evaluated in relation to each other, (2) descriptions of philosophical and social scientific crime and delinquency theories, (3) the presentation of the policy implications of each of the theories, and (4) a comprehensive critique of each of the theories. I hope that students who read this book came to appreciate the diversity of crime and delinquency theories as well as the policy implications and problems associated with each of them.

This second edition, *A Primer on Crime and Delinquency Theory,* has remained faithful to the first in both intent and organization. However, its content has been increased, though it remains a relatively thin volume. New material has been added to every chapter to either clarify or expand explanations in the first edition, include material omitted, or describe developments since the first edition was completed about four years ago. A list of some the new material is provided in the text that follows. A second change is the addition of study questions to the end of each chapter. The study questions are intended to promote class discussion and can also be used for examination purposes. Note that the study questions at the end of chapters 6 and 7 are divided into sections that correspond to the section headings in the chapters. Students and instructors may want to utilize the questions as they complete each section instead of waiting until they complete the entire chapter. Another suggestion: Do not overlook the endnotes. Not only do they provide sources of information, but they also provide substantive comments and observations that augment material in the text.

Following is a list of some of the second edition's new or expanded topics or issues (with the chapter in which the addition is found in parentheses):

- The politics of all crime and delinquency theories, and the ways policy implications are linked to political views (Chap. 1)

- Nonscientific ways of knowing (Chap. 1)

- The two ontological assumptions on which all crime and delinquency theories are based (Chap. 1)

- The relationship between ethical and metaphysical assumptions (Chap. 1)

- Luminaries of the Enlightenment and the source of their ideas in Greek or classical philosophy (Chap. 2)

- The claim that classical and rational choice theories are based on circular reasoning and are not able to be falsified (Chap. 2)

- A definition of natural laws (Chap. 3)

- Contributions of the early positivists Guerry and Quetelet (Chap. 3)

- Contributions of Lombroso's students Ferri and Garofalo (Chap. 4)

- Areas of ongoing research in biocriminology (Chap. 4)

- Recent developments in race–IQ–crime theory (Chap. 5)

- Sykes and Matza's neutralization theory (Chap. 5)

- The medical model of crime causation (Chap. 5)

- Additional criticisms of routine activity theory (Chap. 6)

- New developments in anomie theory (Chap. 6)

- Additional criticisms of differential association and other learning theories (Chap. 6)

- Additional policy implications of social control theory (Chap. 6)

- Additional criticisms of social control and self-control theories (Chap. 6)

- Tittle's control balance theory (Chap. 6)

- The role of corporate crime in the development of critical theory (Chap. 7)

- Restorative justice as an alternative to punitive justice (Chap. 7)

- Additional problems with conflict theory (Chap. 7)

- Currie's elements of market societies that breed serious violent crime (Chap. 7)

- Ways that criminal law serves the interests of the ruling class (Chap. 7)

- Additional policy implications of left realism (Chap. 7)

- Henry and Milovanovic's constitutive criminology (Chap. 7)

- New developments in integrated theory (Chap. 8)

I would be remiss in concluding this preface without expressing my profound thanks to the reviewers of both the first and second editions. Reviewers of the first edition were J. Forbes Farmer, Franklin Pierce College; John E. Holman, University of North Texas; Lin Huff-Corzine, University of Central Florida; John W. King, Baldwin Wallace College; Peter C. Kratcoski, Kent State University; Paul E. Lawson, Montana State University; William S. Lofquist, State University of New York at Geneseo; Thomas C. Tomlinson, Western Illinois University; and Allen E. Wagner, University of Missouri at St. Louis. Reviewers of the second edition were Dan Alpert, Wadsworth Publishing Co.; Brandon Applegate, University of Central Florida; Gregg Barak, Eastern Michigan University; Mark Lanier, University of Central Florida; Matt Robinson, Appalachian State University; and Peter Wood, Mississippi State University. I am especially grateful to the reviewers of the second edition whose help was motivated entirely by friendship. I am lucky to have such good friends.

As mentioned in the preface to the first edition of this book, ultimately, I hope that the knowledge gained by studying this thin volume will lead to the significant reduction in the harm and suffering experienced by crime victims and to the improvement of the quality of life.

Robert M. Bohm

1

⊞

An Introduction
to Theory

What Is Theory?

Testing Theories

**Why Is Theory Important, or Why Study Crime and
Delinquency Theory?**

WHAT IS THEORY?

A *theory* is an explanation. It tells why or how things are related to
each other.[1] A theory of crime explains why or how a certain
thing or certain things are related to criminal behavior. For
example, some theories assume that crime is a part of human nature,
that human beings are born evil. In those theories, human nature is the
thing explained in relation to crime. Other theories assume that crime
is caused by biological things (for example, chromosome abnormalities,
hormone imbalances), psychological things (such as below-normal
intelligence, satisfaction of basic needs), sociological things (for instance,
social disorganization, inadequate socialization), economic things (such
as poverty, unemployment), or some combination of all four kinds of
things. In the chapters that follow, a variety of things associated with

crime are examined. (Note that, unless indicated otherwise, the term *crime* includes delinquency.)

Scientific theories are comprised of (1) concepts, (2) definitions of concepts, and (3) propositions. Those "things" mentioned in the previous paragraph, including criminal behavior, are called concepts. *Concepts* are words or phrases that represent some phenomenon in the world. The object of theory is to explain the interrelationship of concepts, that is, how concepts are related to each other. For example, through theory, we might attempt to explain how the concepts of crime and poverty are interrelated. Does poverty cause crime? Does crime cause poverty?

Definitions of concepts refer to both nominal and operational definitions. *Nominal definitions* are "dictionary definitions" assigned to concepts to clarify what the concepts mean to a researcher and to make possible general discussions about them. The generally accepted nominal definition of the concept of crime, for example, is a violation of the criminal law. *Operational definitions* describe how concepts are or will be measured for research purposes. Standard operational definitions of the concept of crime include the category of "offenses known to the police" as reported in the Federal Bureau of Investigation's (FBI's) uniform crime reports or data on victimizations as reported in the U.S. Justice Department's national crime victimization surveys. "Offenses known to the police" refer to crimes that are sometimes discovered by the police, but more generally are reported to the police and officially recorded by the police and sent to the FBI. Data from the national crime victimization surveys are based on interviews in which respondents are asked whether they have been victims of certain crimes during the past six months, and if they have, they are asked to provide information about the experience. Most crime theories assume those nominal and operational definitions. Only interactionist, radical, and some critical theories question their usage. Still, debates about what should or should not be considered a violation of the criminal law and, hence, a crime, continue among academicians, politicians, and the public.[2]

Interrelated concepts are called *propositions*. An example of a proposition that interrelates the concepts of poverty and crime is: "As poverty increases, crime increases." This particular relationship is referred to as a *positive linear relationship*. A positive linear relationship is one in which concepts increase or decrease together in a relatively straight-line fashion. Using the concepts of poverty and crime as examples, a positive linear relationship would be one where both poverty and crime increase or decrease together in a relatively straight-line fashion.

A *negative linear relationship* is one in which concepts vary in opposite directions in a relatively straight-line fashion. Thus, using the concepts of poverty and crime again, a negative linear relationship would be one where poverty increases while crime decreases or poverty decreases while crime increases.

Possibly no relationship exists between the concepts. For example, poverty and crime may be completely unrelated to each other. In other words, increases or decreases in poverty may have no relationship to crime whatsoever.

Finally, not all relationships are linear. An example of a nonlinear relationship, using the concepts of poverty and crime, is that as poverty increases to a point, crime also increases, but after poverty reaches that point, crime decreases. This is called a *curvilinear relationship*, and some criminologists believe that it describes the relationship between poverty and crime during the height of the Depression in the United States during the 1930s.[3]

All theories are based on certain philosophical assumptions or ideas that cannot be tested scientifically or empirically.[4] A *scientific* or *empirical test* is one that uses the human senses (seeing, hearing, smelling, tasting, and touching) to discover some aspect of the world. Philosophical assumptions are like religion in a way—they are either believed or they are not, but they cannot be proven empirically or scientifically. For example, despite some arguments to the contrary, it cannot be proven scientifically or empirically that God or a Supreme Being exists. The existence of God or a Supreme Being is either believed or it is not.

Though they often are ignored and thus are sometimes considered the "hidden agenda" of theories, the philosophical assumptions on which all theories are based should be considered another component of all theories. Three types of philosophical assumptions are important to all theories: ethical, epistemological, and metaphysical. *Ethical assumptions* or *normative implications* are ideas about what is "good" and "bad," "right" and "wrong," and what we ought to do. Thus, implicit in each theory about crime are certain value judgments and policy implications that follow logically from the theory. For example, if someone believes that criminal behavior is caused by poverty, then that person is probably making an implicit value judgment that crime and poverty are "bad." A policy implication would be to reduce poverty in an effort to reduce crime. Likewise, if someone believes that criminal behavior is caused by poor parenting, then that person is probably making an implicit value judgment that crime and poor parenting are "bad." A policy implication of the theory would be to reduce crime by improving parenting skills.

Policy implications, whatever they may be, generally can be linked to conservative, liberal, or radical political views. In this way, all crime and delinquency theories are "political." As conventionally defined, conservative policies aim to preserve old or traditional social institutions, methods, customs, and so forth; liberal policies seek reform or change by means of existing social institutions; and radical policies favor fundamental or extreme change by abolishing existing social institutions and creating new ones. Examples of social institutions are the family, organized religion, schools, the media, the political system, and the economic system. Thus, politically conservative criminal justice policies invariably focus on the individual offender, leaving social institutions untouched. Examples of such policies are most bio- or psychotherapeutic interventions, "three strikes and you're out" laws, and the death penalty. Politically liberal criminal justice policies, on the other hand, generally attack crime using existing social institutions, especially agencies of the state. Examples include educational and vocational programs, community policing, and "midnight basketball." Politically radical criminal justice policies, by contrast, seek the fundamental transformation of social institutions or their abolition. An economic system based predominately on socialist rather than capitalist principles, a redefinition of crime, greater attention to corporate and government crimes, and community-based strategies for controlling crime and delinquency are examples of politically radical criminal justice policies. In the examination of crime and delinquency theories throughout this book, the value judgments and policy implications of the theories are described too.

Epistemology is the theory of knowledge. *Epistemological assumptions* address the question of how knowledge is obtained. Most crime and delinquency theories are based on the epistemological assumption that the world can be understood through science, that is, the human capacity to observe and to reason. Other potential ways of knowing include: (1) authority; (2) instinct; (3) introspection; (4) intuition; (5) mysticism; (6) spiritualism; (7) extrasensory perception; (8) anamnesis (recollection from previous lifetimes); (9) supernatural revelation; (10) occult sources, such as astrology; (11) pragmatism; and (12) linguistic analysis.[5]

A further assumption implicit in many crime and delinquency theories is that if the world and its functioning can be understood, then they can be changed. However, other theories of crime and delinquency are based on the epistemological assumption that questions the existence of an objective reality apart from people's imaginations. In this view, each person constructs a somewhat unique social reality. Still other theories of crime and delinquency are based on other epistemological assumptions. In the examination of the theories in this book, the epistemological assumptions of each theory or group of theories are described as well.

Finally, implicit in all theories are *metaphysical assumptions*. Metaphysical assumptions address the question of what is the nature of reality. For purposes of this analysis, the important metaphysical assumptions involve human nature (*ontology*) and the nature of society (*cosmology*). All crime and delinquency theories are based on two ontological assumptions. The first addresses whether human behavior, including criminal behavior, is freewilled or determined. The second considers the inherent condition of human beings, or the condition of human beings in a hypothetical "state of nature."

Some theories assume that human beings are free to do whatever they please, while other theories assume that human beings are determined by forces largely beyond their control. An important corollary of the first assumption is that if humans are freewilled, then they are responsible for their behavior, unless, as is the case in many legal systems, they can provide an acceptable defense or excuse. A corollary of the second assumption is that if behavior is determined, then people ought not to be held liable, or at least not fully liable, for their crimes. If people freely choose to commit crimes and, thus, are responsible for them, then a normative implication is that people should be deterred from committing crimes. However, if criminal behavior is a product of factors (whether biological, psychological, or sociological) largely beyond an individual's control, then an ethical implication is that those factors should be changed or eliminated. Ontological assumptions about free will and determinism will be discussed more fully when specific theories are examined in later chapters of this book.

The inherent condition of human beings, or the condition of human beings in a hypothetical "state of nature," is the second important ontological assumption implicit in all crime and delinquency theories. Three competing conceptualizations differentiate those theories. The first and oldest is that human beings are inherently bad or evil and, thus, likely or expected to commit crime. This view probably originated with the Christian belief that everyone is born into original sin. The seventeenth-century English philosopher Thomas Hobbes (1588–1679), who wrote "the life of man is solitary, poor, nasty, brutish, and short," promoted the idea. This view of human nature is also found in Freudian psychoanalytic theory and some versions of social control theory. If, indeed, human beings are inherently bad or evil, then the general policy implication is that society must devise methods to constrain or control such behavior.

The second conceptualization is attributed to the seventeenth-century English philosopher John Locke (1632–1704) who believed that human beings were born with a "tabula rasa" or blank slate. Such individuals are neither inherently good nor bad, but rather a product of their experiences. Learning theories are based on this assumption. The general policy implication is to structure society to promote experiences conducive to law-abiding behavior rather than criminal behavior.

The third conceptualization portrays human beings as inherently good. This view is associated with the eighteenth-century French philosopher Jean Jacques Rousseau (1712–1778) and forms the basis of most critical theories. If, in this view, human beings are inherently good, then society, or something about society, makes human beings bad and prone to commit crime. The normative implication is to change society so that human beings will not be subjected to corrupting influences.

As for cosmological assumptions, some theories assume that the world is characterized primarily by a consensus about moral values, whereas other theories assume that the world is characterized primarily by conflict about moral values. In the first view, it is assumed that most people agree most of the time about what is right and wrong or good and bad. In the second view, the assumption is that most people disagree most of the time about what is right and wrong or good and bad. If a moral consensus in society exists, then an important ethical issue is how to control conflict. On the other hand, if conflict better characterizes social relations, then building consensus, better appreciating diversity, or repressing dissent and conflict are critical social goals implied by the assumption. Note that ethical assumptions or normative implications are derived directly from metaphysical assumptions. Put differently, beliefs about human nature and the nature of society inevitably guide public policy decisions. As was the case with the other philosophical assumptions, the metaphysical assumptions of each theory or group of theories will be described also.

The philosophical assumptions of theories are important because theories frequently are accepted or rejected because of the belief in a theory's philosophical assumptions rather than on the scientific support (or lack of support) for the theory. A principal reason for this state of affairs is that scientific research into the causes of crime almost never offers a critical test that supports one competing theory over another. Focusing on philosophical assumptions, then, if it is believed that human beings are freewilled and thus completely responsible for their behavior, then it may be difficult to accept theories that posit that crime is determined by factors largely beyond the individual's control. Even when the scientific evidence is compelling, the theory still may be rejected because it is not based on the philosophical assumptions in which one believes.

Philosophical assumptions are often grouped together in organizing schemes called *paradigms*.[6] In this book the theories presented are grouped into three general paradigms: (1) the classical/neoclassical, (2) the positivist, and (3) the critical. The philosophical assumptions associated with each of the paradigms are described as each paradigm is introduced.

TESTING THEORIES

Another important issue is the testing of theories, determining whether one theory is better (has more explanatory power) than another. *Explanatory power*, as applied to theories of crime, refers to the ability of a theory about crime to explain and predict crime in different places at different times. It also refers to a theory's ability to explain many different types of crime (for example, street crime, corporate crime, government crime, organized crime, and so forth) and to explain them at different levels of analysis.[7] A better theory, in other words, provides compelling explanations not only for why individuals commit various crimes but also for rates of crime among various groups.[8] A less compelling theory, by contrast, may provide an explanation at only one level of analysis (for instance, at the individual level or the group level). Explanatory power also is called the *generalizability* or *scope of a theory*, and theories often are judged by this criterion: The greater the explanatory power, generalizability, or scope of a theory, the better the theory.

As noted, scientific theories can be tested scientifically or empirically. However, to call a theory unscientific is not necessarily to condemn it. To call a theory unscientific only means that the theory cannot claim what "good" scientific theories can claim—that the evidence of the senses makes it irrational to reject it. Yet, we should remember that evidence from the senses might be wrong, as in the cases of hallucinations and optical illusions.

Scientific theories are tested through the processes of verification and falsification. *Verification* involves the observation and confirmation of a theoretical proposition's predicted relationship. For example, to verify the proposition that as poverty increases, crime increases, concomitant increases in poverty and crime must be observable and observed. *Falsification* involves disproving a proposition by the observation of negative examples. Thus, given the aforementioned proposition, if it were observed that in some place at some time, poverty increased, while crime decreased, then the proposition and theory of which it is a part would have to be questioned. Finding negative examples for a proposition does not necessarily condemn it, but it does suggest that the theory's explanatory power is limited. The limitation may be a function of the unique historical circumstances in which the theory is produced because most theories are products of their times. When evaluating theories, therefore, it is important to consider the historical context in which the theory emerged. Generally, a theory with greater explanatory power, generalizability, or scope is a more valuable theory.

For most social scientists, falsification is the more critical test of a theory. The principal reason for this is that theories can *never* be proven true, but they can be falsified. Theories can never be proven true because there is always the possibility that an observed relationship may be a function of some other, unconsidered factor. To illustrate, consider the very strong positive relationship between the sale of ice cream and the homicide rate: As the sale of ice cream increases, the homicide rate increases and vice versa. Does this mean that ice cream sales cause homicide? Of course not! What it means is that both the sale of ice cream and the homicide rate are related to a third factor that causes both to increase or decrease together. As one might guess, that third factor is the temperature. As it gets hotter, both ice cream sales and homicides increase; when it gets cooler, both decrease. The relationship between the sale of ice cream and the homicide rate (and it is a real relationship) is called a *spurious relationship*. Because of the potential for spurious relationships, most social scientists consider falsification the hallmark of the scientific method.

When theory is evaluated, then, all that accurately can be said is that one theory is more or less compelling, believable, or convincing than another theory. What makes one theory more compelling, believable, or convincing than another theory is that the more compelling theory has successfully withstood more attempts to falsify it than has the less compelling theory. It is not accurate to say that a theory is true or false or right or wrong.

WHY IS THEORY IMPORTANT, OR WHY STUDY CRIME AND DELINQUENCY THEORY?

Everything people do in life is based on theory. However, many people often are not conscious or aware of the theory that they are using. Nevertheless, whatever they do, they do for a reason. Similarly, everything that is done in criminal justice is based on theory, although most people are unaware of the theory on which those actions are based. Theory is studied, then, to explain and understand why people do what they do. People who are uninterested in theory are people who move blindly through life or, in the case of criminal justice, intervene in other people's lives with only vague notions about why they are doing what they do.

This book focuses on theories of crime and delinquency. Theories of crime and delinquency are studied in an attempt to understand why people commit criminal and delinquent acts. The ultimate goal of this endeavor is to reduce crime and delinquency,[9] but, without a great amount of luck, that goal will only be accomplished by means of a clear theoretical understanding of the problem.

STUDY QUESTIONS

1. What is theory?
2. What are the components of theory?
3. Can a theory be proven true? If yes, how? If not, why not?
4. How are theories judged or evaluated in relation to each other?
5. Why is theory important?

NOTES

1. Much of the discussion in this chapter is from Kerlinger (1964) and Babbie (1992).

2. Although some of the controversy over the definition of crime is described in parts of this book, to keep the book "a primer," a thorough examination of the subject, which, itself, would require a book-length treatment, is regrettably omitted.

3. See, for example, Wilson and Herrnstein (1985:436).

4. See Gouldner (1971) who refers to philosophical assumptions as "background" and "domain assumptions"; also see Einstadter and Henry (1995) whose work focuses on these assumptions.

5. Montague (1953:34); Brennan (1953:164); Mead (1959:150–186); Chisholm (1966); Honer and Hunt (1968:55–75); Christian (1977:180–181).

6. A paradigm is "a fundamental image of the subject matter within a science. It serves to define what should be studied, what questions should be asked, how they should be asked, and what rules should be followed in interpreting the answers obtained. The paradigm is the broadest unit of consensus within a science and serves to differentiate one scientific community ('or subcommunity') from another. It subsumes, defines, and interrelates the exemplars, theories, and methods and

instruments that exist within it." (Ritzer, 1975:7)

7. Tittle (1995:Chap. 2) argues that theories should be evaluated in relation to their *breath* (their capacity to explain a wide range of criminal behaviors), *comprehensiveness* (their inclusion of all possible variables, especially those dealing with motivation, opportunity, ability, constraint, and absence of alternative motivation), *precision* (their ability to specify the operation, form, and contingencies of the causal relationships, such as the time-interval between cause and effect or the influence of extraneous or intervening factors), and *depth* (their ability to show how the causal variables are logically linked to form a meaningful and systematic whole).

8. Theories of why individuals commit crimes are sometimes referred to as *microtheories* or *process theories*. Theories that explain rates of crime among various groups are sometimes called *macrotheories* or *structural theories*.

9. Actually, the ultimate goal of this project is to improve the quality of life, the effort toward which, it is assumed, can be aided by the reduction of socially harmful behaviors, whether legally defined as criminal or not.

2

Classical and Neoclassical Theory

Classical theory is a product of the philosophy of the Enlightenment, a period of social history roughly spanning the time of transition between the Protestant Reformation (1517) and the American and French Revolutions (1776 and 1789, respectively). The Enlightenment, or the "Age of Reason," was characterized by an intellectual challenge to the then-dominant theological worldview and theologically derived knowledge based on revelation and the authority of the Church.

During the "Dark Ages," the nearly thousand years between the fall of the western Roman Empire (476) and the Reformation, theology constituted the source of virtually all knowledge. The Church dominated both humankind and society, as Carl Becker, a noted philosopher, describes:

> Existence was . . . regarded by the medieval man as a cosmic drama, composed by the master dramatist according to a central theme and on a rational plan. . . . The duty of man was to accept the drama as written, since he could not alter it; his function, to play the role assigned. That he might play his role according to the divine text, subordinate authorities—church and state—deriving their just powers from the will of God, were instituted among men to dispose them to submission and to instruct them in their proper lines.[1]

The challenge to the theologically based worldview and the authority of the Church came from Enlightenment thinkers who promoted a new, "scientific" worldview based on reason. For Enlightenment thinkers, who drew many of their ideas from the Greek or "classical" philosophers Socrates (469–399 B.C.), Plato (427–347 B.C.), and Aristotle (384–322 B.C.), reason, especially in those areas where personal observation was possible, was a legitimate and more democratic source of knowledge. Reason, for Enlightenment thinkers, referred to either the rationalism of Thomas Hobbes (1588–1679), Rene Descartes (1596–1650), Benedict de Spinoza (1632–1677), John Locke (1632–1704), Gottfried Wilhelm Leibniz (1646–1716), Francois Marie Arouet de Voltaire (1694–1778), Charles de Secondat, the Baron de Montesquieu (1689–1755), Jean Jacques Rousseau (1712–1778), and others, or the empiricism of Francis Bacon (1561–1626), Galileo Galilei (1564–1642), Johann Kepler (1571–1630), and Isaac Newton (1642–1727), among others.[2]

As noted, the new, scientific worldview of the Enlightenment thinkers explicitly rejected the theological worldview, considering it a fraud or at least an illusion. Again, as Carl Becker explains:

> Renunciation of the traditional revelation was the very condition of being truly enlightened; for to be truly enlightened was to see the light in all its fullness, and the light in its fullness revealed two very simple and obvious facts . . . the fact that the supposed revelation of God's purposes through Holy Writ and Holy Church was a fraud, or at best an illusion born of ignorance, perpetrated, or at least maintained, by the priests in order to accentuate the fears of mankind, and so hold it in subjection. The other . . . that God had revealed his purpose to men in a far more simple and natural, a far less mysterious and recondite way, through his works. To be enlightened was to understand this double truth, that it was not in Holy Writ, but in the great book of nature, open for all mankind to read, that the laws of God had been recorded. This is the new revelation, and thus at last we enter the secret door to knowledge.[3]

The Enlightenment thinkers assumed that human beings could understand the world through science—the human capacity to observe and reason. Moreover, they believed that if the world and its functioning could be understood, then it also could be changed. They rejected the belief that either the world or the people in it were divinely ordained or determined.

Instead, they believed that people were *freewilled* and thus completely responsible for their actions. Human behavior was considered motivated by a *hedonistic rationality* (Bentham's "felicity calculus") where actors weighed the potential pleasure of an action against the possible pain associated with it. Human beings committed crime, in this view, because they rationally calculated that the crime would give them more pleasure than pain. Before the Enlightenment, crime was equated with sin and was considered the work of demons or the Devil.[4] Among the Enlightenment thinkers associated with the classical school of criminology were: Cesare Bonesana, the Marchese de Beccaria (1738–1794) of Italy, Jeremy Bentham (1748–1832), William Blackstone (1723–1780), John Howard (1726–1790), and Samuel Romilly (1757–1818)—all of England—and Paul Johann Anselm von Feurbach (1775–1883) of Germany.

In the realm of criminal justice, horrible and severe punishments were common both before and during the Enlightenment. For example, in England during the eighteenth century, almost 150 offenses carried the death penalty.[5] Consider the following account of the punishment of Damiens, who in 1757 stabbed, but did not kill, King Louis XV of France:

> At seven o'clock in the morning of his execution day, Damiens was led to the torture chamber, where his legs were placed in "boots" that were squeezed gradually as wedges were inserted. A total of eight wedges were inserted, each at fifteen-minute intervals, until the attending physicians warned that an additional wedge could provoke an "accident" [Damiens' premature death]. Thereupon, Damiens was removed to the place where he would be executed. . . . The condemned man was placed on a scaffold, where a rope was tied to each arm and leg. Then, Damiens' hand was burned with a brazier containing burning sulphur, after which red-hot tongs were used to pinch his arms, thighs, and chest. Molten lead and boiling oil were poured onto his open wounds several times, and after each time the prisoner screamed in agony. Next, four huge horses were whipped by attendants as they pulled the ropes around Damiens' bleeding wounds for an hour. Only after some of the tendons were cut did two legs and one arm separate from Damiens' torso. He remained alive and breathing until the second arm was cut from his body. All parts of Damiens' body were hurled into a nearby fire for burning.[6]

The classicists, as Enlightenment thinkers, were concerned with protecting the rights of humankind from the corruption and excesses of the existing legal institutions.[7] Arbitrary and barbarous punishments were not the only problems. At the time, crime itself was poorly defined and extensive. Due process of law was either absent or ignored. For example, people could be arrested without warrants and be held in custody indefinitely without knowing why they were being held. Torture was routinely employed to extract confessions. Judgeships typically were sold to wealthy persons by the sovereign, and judges had almost total discretion.

It was within that historical context that Beccaria wrote and published anonymously in 1764 his truly revolutionary work, *On Crimes and Punishments* (*Dei Delitti e delle Pene*). His book generally is acknowledged to have had "more practical effect than any other treatise ever written in the long campaign against barbarism in criminal law and procedure."[8] Historians of criminal law credit Beccaria's arguments with ending legal torture throughout Christendom.[9] At the time, however, Beccaria's treatise was not universally acclaimed. For example, in 1765, the Pope placed Beccaria's work on a list of banned books for its "extreme rationalism."[10] Nevertheless, in the book, Beccaria sets forth most of what we now call classical criminological theory.

According to Beccaria, the only justified rationale for laws and punishments is the principle of *utility*, that is, "the greatest happiness shared by the greatest number."[11] For Beccaria, "Laws are the conditions under which independent and isolated men united to form a society."[12] Criminal law should be based on positive sanction; that is, every member of society has a right to do anything that is not prohibited by law, without fearing anything but natural consequences. The source of law should be the legislature and not judges.

Beccaria believed that the basis of society, as well as the origin of punishments and the right to punish, is the *social contract*.[13] The social contract is an imaginary agreement entered into by persons who have sacrificed the minimum amount of their liberty necessary to prevent what the English philosopher Hobbes called "the war of all against all." In describing the social contract, Beccaria wrote:

> Weary of living in a continual state of war, and of enjoying a liberty rendered useless by the uncertainty of preserving it, they [people] sacrificed a part so that they might enjoy the rest of it in peace and safety. The sum of all these portions of liberty sacrificed by each for his own good constitutes the sovereignty of a nation, and their legitimate depository and administrator is the sovereign.[14]

However, Beccaria realized that establishing the social contract is not enough to prevent people from infringing on the remaining liberties of other people. Thus, Beccaria believed that punishment is necessary.

For Beccaria, the only legitimate purpose for punishment is deterrence, both special and general.[15] *Special* or *specific deterrence* is the prevention of particular individuals from committing crime again by punishing them, while *general deterrence* is the prevention of people in general or society at large from engaging in crime by punishing specific individuals and making examples of them. Beccaria summarized his position on punishment in the following way: "In order for punishment not to be, in every instance, an act of violence of one or of many against a private citizen, it must be essentially public, prompt, necessary, the least possible in the given circumstances, proportionate to the crime, dictated by the laws."[16]

It is important to emphasize that Beccaria promoted crime prevention over punishment. As Beccaria maintained, "It is better to prevent crimes than to punish them. This is the ultimate end of every good legislation [that is, to lead] men to the greatest possible happiness or the least possible unhappiness."[17] Beccaria recommended six ways to prevent crimes:[18]

1. Social contract
2. Law (must be clear, simple, unbiased, and reflect the consensus of the entire population)
3. Punishment (must be proportionate to the crime, prompt and certain, public, necessary, and dictated by the laws and not judges' discretion)
4. Education (enlightenment): "Knowledge breeds evil in inverse ratio to its diffusion, and benefits in direct ratio."
5. Eliminate corruption from the administration of justice
6. Reward virtue

In sum, Beccaria's main ideas are as follows: Human motivation is governed by a rational hedonism. A society based on a social contract is necessary to escape criminal violence and other predatory behavior. The state has the right to punish. Penalties should be legislated, with a scale of crimes and punishments. It is better to prevent crimes than to punish them.

A contemporary version of classical theory is *rational choice theory*, developed most fully by Cornish and Clarke.[19] In this theory, it is assumed that, before many people commit crimes, they consider the risks and rewards. Economists have presented a more quantitative version of rational choice theory in their attempt to explain criminal behavior through a costs and benefits analysis.[20] The costs and benefits may be either material (for example, money) or psychological.

The classical school has been characterized as legal and administrative criminology[21] and denounced as "armchair criminology."[22] Its application was supposed to make the criminal law fairer and easier to administer. To those ends, judicial discretion would be eliminated.

Judges would only determine innocence or guilt. All offenders would be treated alike, and similar crimes would be treated similarly. Individual differences among offenders and unique or mitigating circumstances about the crime would be ignored. A problem is that all offenders are not alike and similar crimes are not always as similar as they might appear on the surface. Should first offenders be treated the same as habitual offenders? Should juveniles be treated the same as adults? Should the insane be treated the same as the sane? Should a crime of passion be treated the same as the intentional commission of a crime? The classical school's answer to all of those difficult questions would be a simple yes.

The theory of the classical school of criminology poses other problems as well. For example, classical theory assumes that there is a consensus in society, at least about the desirability of a social contract.[23] However, as much as it may be in everyone's interest to be protected from criminal violence, in a society in which the distribution of property is inequitable, it may not be in everyone's interest to have the present distribution of property protected. Why would a person without property agree to enter into a social contract to protect the existing distribution of property?

Classical theory also assumes that rational people will choose to enter into the social contract; thus, anyone who commits crime is pathological or irrational, that is, unable or unwilling to enter into a social contract.[24] Again, why would a person without property want to enter into a social contract to protect the existing distribution of property? Classical theory fails to consider that crime may be rational given the individual's social position.[25] On the other hand, classical theory, especially rational choice theory and economic models, has been criticized for overemphasizing the degree to which offenders rationally calculate the consequences of their actions.[26]

Placed in its historical context, classical theory turns out to be an ideological justification for the position of the then new and increasingly prosperous merchant or business class.[27] Beccaria's system of justice protected the newly propertied classes, while controlling all others, especially the old landed aristocracy who was in direct political competition with the new merchant or business class. Although Beccaria was born a member of the aristocracy as a marquis, he had no property and was a disaffected member of his class.[28] Other classical criminologists were members of the new merchant or business class or were in sympathy with them. Note that rational calculation of pains of punishment versus the pleasure of success makes more sense for property crime than for violent crime.

In addition, there were very practical reasons (to the new merchant or business class) for making the laws more humane and reducing capital and corporal punishment. In the first place, under the system of barbarous punishments, judges and juries were frequently reluctant to convict, thus diminishing deterrence. By reducing the severity of punishments, judges and juries were more likely to convict, and, as a result, property was better protected. An added benefit of sending offenders to prison rather than killing or maiming them was that prisons indoctrinated work habits in prisoners (or so it was thought), preparing them for labor in the newly emerging industrial age. It was considered wasteful to destroy able-bodied workers.

Another problem with classical theory is the assumption that human beings are freewilled and completely responsible for their behavior. Among the first Enlightenment thinkers to counter those notions, and take what at the time was a very unpopular position, was the seventeenth-century philosopher Benedict de Spinoza (1632–1677). According to Spinoza, people often believe they are freewilled or choose freely, but this belief is a product of their ignorance of the causes that determine their actions or choices. Thus, as Spinoza concluded, "It is absurd to praise or blame people since they are and do what they must be and do. We should rather seek to understand the causes of their actions and states of mind."[29] Beirne has recently argued that Beccaria has been misinterpreted and that he was "resolutely opposed to any notion of free will."[30] Beirne maintains that Beccaria believed that "human agents are no more than the products of their sensory reactions to external stimuli."[31] Besides, a belief in free will would seem to deny the contributions of all modern social sciences, as well as the success of the entire advertising industry. The sole purpose of the advertising industry, after all, is to create and maintain a market for commodities by manipulating human behavior. Perhaps a more fundamental problem is the apparent contradiction between the ideas of free will and social contract. If people cede a minimum amount of liberty as their share in the social contract, then they are no longer totally free but are minimally constrained by the state to which they ceded their liberty.

Still another problem with classical theory is its belief in deterrence. In the first place, little scientific evidence supports the contention that people do not commit crimes because they are afraid of being punished.[32] Second, even if deterrence exists (and this is not the place to delve into the methodological difficulties of demonstrating why people do *not* act in a given situation), then it probably is effective only for people who have been adequately socialized. How threatened are people whose lives are miserable beyond all hope? What about people ("outsiders") whose value systems are not likely to be changed? For those types of people, deterrence is unlikely to be effective.

Finally, classical theory, as well as both versions of rational choice theory, has been criticized for being based on circular reasoning (people rationally choose to commit crimes and their crimes are evidence of their rational choices) and for being unable to be falsified.[33] Regarding the latter, how is it possible to falsify the claim that criminal behavior was rational for the person who committed it?

Despite those problems, Beccaria's ideas, as previously noted, were very influential. France, for example, adopted many of Beccaria's principles in its Code of 1791, in particular, the principle of equal punishments for the same crimes. However, because classical theory ignored both individual differences among offenders and mitigating circumstances, applying the law in practice was difficult. Because of that difficulty, as well as new developments in the emerging behavioral sciences, modifications in classical theory and its application were introduced.

Several modifications of classical theory collectively are referred to as *neoclassical theory*.[34] The principal difference between the two theories has to do with classical theory's assumptions about free will. In the neoclassical revision, it was conceded that certain factors (for example, insanity) might inhibit the exercise of free will.[35] Thus, the idea of premeditation was introduced as a measure of the degree of free will exercised.[36] Also, mitigating circumstances were considered legitimate grounds for an argument of diminished responsibility.[37]

Those modifications of classical theory, as embodied in the revised French Code of 1819, had two practical effects. First, they provided a reason for nonlegal experts (such as medical doctors) to testify in court as to the degree of diminished responsibility of an offender.[38] Second, offenders began to be sentenced to punishments that were considered rehabilitative.[39] The idea was that certain environments were more conducive than others to the exercise of rational choice.[40] However, consistent with the classical school's implicit ideology about the sanctity of preserving the distribution of private property, the modifications in the theory that were made conspicuously omitted consideration of economic pressure as a mitigating circumstance and a legal excuse for criminal responsibility.

In any event, the reason so much emphasis has been placed on the classical school of criminology and its neoclassical revisions is that together they are essentially the model on which criminal justice in the United States is based today. During the past quarter of a century, at least in part because of dissatisfaction with the exercise of judicial discretion, determinate and mandatory sentences based on sentencing guidelines have all but replaced indeterminate sentences. In addition, a similar dissatisfaction with the discretion exercised by parole boards has led to the abolition of parole in the federal jurisdiction and in some states.

The revival of classical theory during the past twenty-five years also is probably the result of a perceived failure on the part of criminologists to discover the causes of crime. In a renewed effort to deter crimes, judges currently are sentencing more offenders to prison for longer periods than at any other time in the history of the United States, and some states are again using capital punishment. Ironically, one reason the theory of the classical school lost favor in the nineteenth century was the belief that punishment was not a particularly effective method of preventing or controlling crime.[41]

STUDY QUESTIONS

1. What is the cause of crime from the perspective of the classical school (including contemporary versions)?

2. How would classical theorists prevent crime?

3. What are problems with the theory of the classical school?

4. What changes or modifications to classical theory did the neoclassicists make? Why?

NOTES

1. Becker (1932:7).

2. Zeitlin (1968:Chap. 1). Rationalism is based on *deductive logic*, which involves reasoning from the general to the particular; conclusions are drawn from one or more given premises. Empiricism, on the other hand, is based on *inductive logic*, which involves reasoning from the particular to the general; conclusions are drawn about all members of a group from observation of only some of them. The preceding definitions are from Runes (1968); Babbie (1992). Put differently, in deduction the scientist reasons (that is, theorizes or creates hypotheses) and then observes, using the observations to support or refute the hypotheses and theory, whereas in

induction the scientist observes then reasons, using the observations to create theory and testable hypotheses. Modern scientific reasoning frequently combines deduction and induction.

3. Becker (1932:50–51).

4. Some still hold this view today.

5. Bohm (1999:2); Thompson (1975:22–23); Bedau (1982:7).

6. From Jones (1987:26); also see Foucault (1977:3–6) for a somewhat different description of the same event.

7. Taylor et al. (1974:1).

8. Beccaria (1975:ix).

9. Beccaria (1975:ix).

10. Beirne (1991:782).

11. Beccaria (1975:8).

12. Beccaria (1975:11).

13. The English philosophers Hobbes (1588–1679) and Locke (1632–1704) wrote about the social contract in the seventeenth century, and the French philosopher Rousseau (1712–1778) wrote about the social contract in a book published in 1762—two years before the publication of Beccaria's *On Crimes and Punishments.*

14. Beccaria (1975:11–12).

15. Beccaria (1975:42).

16. Beccaria (1975:99).

17. Beccaria (1975:93).

18. Beccaria (1975:94–95).

19. Cornish and Clarke (1986).

20. See Curran and Renzetti (1994:20).

21. Vold (1958:23).

22. Curran and Renzetti (1994:22).

23. See Taylor et al. (1974:3).

24. Taylor et al. (1974:3); but see Vold and Bernard (1986:28–29) for a different view.

25. See Taylor et al. (1974:3).

26. Curran and Renzetti (1994:21); Tittle (1995:12).

27. Taylor et al. (1974:3).

28. Beccaria (1975).

29. Berofsky (1973:238).

30. Beirne (1991:807).

31. Beirne (1991:807).

32. See Paternoster (1987); Finckenauer (1982).

33. Tittle (1995:10–11).

34. See Taylor et al. (1974:7).

35. Vold (1979:28).

36. Vold (1979:28).

37. Vold (1979:28).

38. Taylor et al. (1974:8).

39. Taylor et al. (1974:9).

40. Taylor et al. (1974:9).

41. See Vold and Bernard (1986:33).

3

Positivist Theories

Positive Philosophy

The Influence of Empirical or Experimental Science

**Major Differences between Positivism and
Classicism/Neoclassicism**

General Problems with Positivist Theories

The theories of the positivist school of criminology grew out of positive philosophy and the logic and methodology of empirical or experimental science. Positive philosophy was an explicit repudiation or reaction to the critical and "negative" philosophy of the Enlightenment thinkers.

POSITIVE PHILOSOPHY

Among the founders of the positivist school of thought and, according to some, the first modern sociologist, was Claude Henri, the Count de Saint-Simon (1760–1825). Saint-Simon, who fought with the French army during the American Revolution and supported the French Revolution, hated the anarchy that followed the French Revolution.[1]

Saint-Simon wanted to preserve the status quo, which, at the time for him, was the emerging middle-class society then in process of consolidating itself. He came to oppose radical reform, as manifested by the French Revolution, because he believed that society evolved and that each stage in the evolutionary development of society was necessary and perfect.

Perhaps better known than Saint-Simon is Auguste Comte (1798–1857), who also has been credited with founding sociology.[2] Comte believed that it was impossible to restore the old feudal-theological order that rapidly was being replaced by science and industry. He acknowledged that the Enlightenment thinkers had contributed to progress, in a negative sense, by helping to break up the old system and paving the way for a new one. However, Comte argued that the thought of the Enlightenment had outlived its usefulness and had become obstructive. He rejected the idea that government was the enemy of society and that it was necessary to restrict the activity of government (for example, the exercise of judicial discretion) to guard against its interference.

Comte believed that the idea of free will was nothing more than an article of faith. Although acknowledging its usefulness in the battle against theological authority, he did not think that it was helpful any longer. He maintained that social reorganization required intellectual organization, which was impossible as long as individuals had the right to inquire into subjects about which they knew little. For Comte, social order was not compatible with perpetual discussions about the foundations of society.

He believed that the ideas of equality and of the sovereignty of the people were other erroneous articles of faith and that they condemned superior people to the will of the masses. Comte was no democrat! He viewed social evils as products of ideas and manners and not of basic economic and political institutions. As a result, he maintained that existing institutions must not be altered or changed. He believed that people, especially the lower classes, should be submissive to authority and the "natural laws" and resign themselves to their lot in life—anything else would prove fatal to progress. The *natural laws* are supposed to be based on the core values of civilization, universally valid, discoverable only through reason, and superior to the laws of human beings or the state.[3] The scientific elite would be the final arbiter on what the natural laws were and would indicate to the lower classes how their lot in life may be slowly improved in accordance with those laws. In his *Politique Positive* (1854), Comte unabashedly proclaimed himself Pope of the new positive religion.

In sum, positive philosophy was based on the idea that science had no other aim than the establishment of intellectual order, which, it was assumed, is the basis of every other order. The purpose of positive philosophy was to avert revolution and achieve the resignation of the masses to the conditions of the existing order. Politically, positive philosophy is extremely conservative.

THE INFLUENCE OF EMPIRICAL
OR EXPERIMENTAL SCIENCE

Publication of the first modern national crime statistics in France in 1827, together with official records of economic conditions, which became available in a few European countries in the 1600s, made it possible for positivists such as Andre Michel Guerry (1802–1866) and Adolphe Quetelet (1796–1874) to study empirically the relationship between various economic conditions and crime.[4] In the late 1820s and early 1830s, both Guerry and Quetelet independently analyzed the annually published crime rates and discovered that the rates remained remarkably constant from year to year and that the contribution of various types of crimes to the overall crime rate varied little. From those findings, they concluded that crime must be a regular feature of social life; that crime must be rooted in social arrangements; and, if those arrangements could be identified, crime could be eliminated.

Guerry and Quetelet also used available statistics to examine the intuitively appealing proposition that poverty caused crime. Again, working independently, they found that the relationship was more complex than they originally believed. For example, they found higher rates of property crimes, but lower rates of violent crimes, in the wealthiest regions of France. Guerry concluded that poverty itself was not the cause of property crime. Instead, he pointed to opportunity as the culprit, arguing that in wealthier areas there was more to steal. Quetelet, who analyzed data from Belgium and Holland in addition to France, agreed with Guerry that opportunity was a cause of property crime. However, Quetelet also suggested that "relative poverty," where there is great inequality between poverty and wealth in the same area, also played a key role in both property and violent crimes. According to Quetelet, relative poverty incites people through jealousy to commit crimes. This is especially true where changing economic conditions cause the impoverishment of some people while others retain their wealth. Quetelet found less crime in poor areas than in wealthier areas as long as the people in the poor areas were still able to satisfy their basic needs. In short, Guerry and Quetelet were among the first social scientists (they were called "moral statisticians") to use empirical analysis to show that crime was related to social arrangements.

Also key to the development of positivism were new discoveries in biology. Especially important were findings that led to the identification of human beings with the rest of the animal world.[5] In the *Descent of Man* (1871), Charles Darwin (1809–1882) suggested that some people were "less highly evolved or developed than others"; some people "were nearer their ape-like ancestors than others in traits, abilities, and dispositions."[6]

At about the same time, experimentation with animals was becoming an increasingly accepted way of learning about human beings in physiology, medicine, psychology, and psychiatry.[7] Human beings were beginning to appear to science as one of many creatures, with no special connection to God.[8] Human beings were beginning to be understood, not as freewilled, self-determining creatures who could do anything that they wanted to do, but rather as beings whose action was determined by biological and cultural factors.[9]

MAJOR DIFFERENCES
BETWEEN POSITIVISM
AND CLASSICISM/NEOCLASSICISM

First, positivists assume that human behavior is determined and not a matter of free will.[10] Consequently, positivists focus on cause-and-effect relationships. Causation is established when three conditions are met: (1) the presumed cause precedes the presumed effect in time, (2) the presumed cause and the presumed effect are empirically correlated with one another, and (3) the observed empirical correlation between the presumed cause and the presumed effect is not spurious—that is, the empirical relationship cannot be explained away as being due to the influence of some other factor or factors.[11]

It is important to note that the ontological debate in philosophy over whether human beings are "freewilled" or "determined" is an ancient one. However, neither position seems to capture the way most people experience or interpret their behavior. To partially resolve the dilemma, many social scientists distinguish between a "hard" and a "soft" determinism. *Hard determinism* refers to an all-encompassing compulsion; human beings have no choices whatsoever when confronting situations. *Soft determinism*, a concept that has been attributed to the American philosopher William James (1842–1910) and has also been referred to as "conditional free will,"[12] allows for constrained choice. That is, in any circumstance human beings always have choices, however limited they may be. The most limited choice is to act or not to act. Generally, the more choices people have, the greater the "freedom" they experience. (This notion is what many social scientists mean by "freedom.") The number of choices people have also is an important indicator of social status: the more choices, the higher the status. Thus, rather than making a distinction between free will and determinism, the distinction made by most social scientists is between hard and soft determinism.

A second difference is that positivists assume that criminals are fundamentally different from noncriminals, either biologically, psychologically, sociologically, or in some combination of all three.[13] Positivists search for such differences by scientific methods.[14] When differences are found, classifications or categories, such as criminal and noncriminal, are created. Classical criminologists, on the other hand, assumed that there are no fundamental differences between people who commit crimes and those who do not. People who choose to commit crimes simply have the opportunity and calculate that the crimes will bring them more pleasure than not committing them or getting caught and punished.

Third, positivists assume that social scientists, including criminologists, can be objective or value-neutral in their work.[15] Comte, for example, chided classical theorists about their attempts to comprehend and reason about reality without supporting their contentions with facts. (More will be said about this problem in the next section.)

Fourth, positivists frequently assume that crime is caused by multiple factors, such as hormone imbalances, below-normal intelligence, inadequate socialization or self-control, and economic inequality.[16] Classical criminologists, as noted previously, assumed that crime is caused by individuals who freely choose to commit it after rationally calculating that the crime will provide them more pleasure than pain. (Neoclassical theorists conceded that some individuals might commit crimes because their free will and rational calculating ability are impaired.)

Fifth, positivists believe that society is based primarily on a consensus about moral values but not on a social contract, as classical theorists believed. Rather, for most postivists, social consensus is a product of either Durkheim's collective conscience (that is, the general sense of morality of the times) in more primitive or homogeneous societies or his interdependency of occupational roles (that is, the division of labor) in more advanced societies. (Both of those concepts are described in greater detail in Chapter 6.)[17]

GENERAL PROBLEMS
WITH POSITIVIST THEORIES

Although there are problems peculiar to each positivist theory of crime causation, some of which will be described as the biological, psychological, and sociological theories are examined, problems generic to the theories as a group also arise. In this section, five of these general problems are presented. It is important to remember, as discussed in Chapter 1, that these problems do not necessarily condemn a theory. They only diminish the theory's explanatory power.

First is the problem of overprediction.[18] Positivist theories generally account for too much crime. At the same time, they do not explain exceptions well. For example, in a theory that suggests that crime is caused by poverty, the theory overpredicts because not all poor people commit crime. The theory also cannot explain adequately why many poor people do not commit crimes. Regarding the difficulty in explaining exceptions, positivist theories, especially many sociological theories, generally ignore individual differences. Large groups of people are presumed to respond similarly to the same biological, psychological, and especially sociological factors.

Second, positivist theories generally ignore the criminalization process. They take the legal definition of crime for granted. Ignored is the question why certain behaviors are defined as criminal whereas other, similar behaviors are not. The problem occurs because positivists generally separate the study of crime from a theory of the law and the state.[19]

Third is the problem with the consensual worldview, the belief in a normative consensus.[20] Most positivist theories assume that most people agree most of the time about moral values; that is, general agreement prevails about what is right and wrong and good and bad. The problem with such a view is that it ignores the issue of power, as well as the multitude of fundamental conflicts of value and interest in society. It also denies the existence of multiple and socially constructed realties and leads to a blind acceptance of the status quo.

A fourth problem is the belief in determinism, the idea that choice of action is not free but is determined by causes independent of will.[21] Positivists generally assume that human beings only adapt or react. A problem is that they also create. How else do you explain new social arrangements or new ways of thinking?[22] Even if criminal behavior were determined, identifying the "cause" or "causes" of crime is a problem because establishing a lack of spuriousness (the absence of influential but unconsidered factors) may be impossible.[23]

The belief in determinism allows the positivist to present an absolute situation uncomplicated by the ability to choose.[24] The belief makes rational planning and control logically possible, that is, with the help of the positivist.[25]

A fifth general problem with positivist theories is the belief in the ability of social scientists, including criminologists, to be objective or value-neutral in their work.[26] Assuming that an "objective reality" exists independent of their perception of it, positivists often fail to understand that what they know is a product of how they interpret what they observe. What is observed ultimately depends on an individual's cognitive apparatus, his or her past experiences, as well as the social context in which the observation is made. The problem is that social scientists, as well as all other human beings, are always biased. Human beings are biased by virtue of their being human. To deny this point is self-deception. Why do you suppose social scientists select a particular problem to study? For that matter, why do you suppose that social scientists choose their particular occupation? Perhaps it is because they have an interest in the subject matter. Many positivists fail to recognize that to describe and to evaluate such human action as criminal behavior is fundamentally a moral endeavor and, therefore, subject to bias. Those positivists who do recognize the problem of bias attempt to overcome it. Whether they ever can be successful is another matter.

STUDY QUESTIONS

1. What influence did Saint-Simon and Comte have on the development of positivist theory?

2. What influence did Guerry and Quetelet have on the development of positivist theory?

3. What influence did Darwin have on the development of positivist theory?

4. What are major differences between positivism and classicism/neoclassicism?

5. What are general problems with positivist theories?

NOTES

1. Unless indicated otherwise, material in this section is from Comte (1974); Runes (1968); Saint-Simon (1964), and especially Zeitlin (1968).

2. Vold and Bernard (1986:144).

3. See Runes (1968:206).

4. The following description is from Vold and Bernard (1986: 131–132); Taylor et al. (1974: 37–38).

5. Vold (1979:35).

6. Vold (1979:36).

7. Vold and Bernard (1986:36).

8. Vold and Bernard (1986:36).

9. Vold and Bernard (1986:36).

10. See Taylor et al. (1974:21–23, 31–32); Davis (1975).

11. See Babbie (1992:72).

12. See Fishbein (1990:30–31).

13. See Vold and Bernard (1986:45); Matza (1964:11–12).

14. See Taylor et al. (1974:11).

15. See Taylor et al. (1974:11, 19–21, 26); Davis (1975).

16. See Vold (1979:37, 47).

17. See Taylor et al. (1974:11–19, 31); Davis (1975); Durkheim (1933).

18. See Taylor et al. (1974:24–26); Matza (1964:21–22).

19. See Taylor et al. (1974:28); Matza (1964:5).

20. See Taylor et al. (1974:26–28, 31); Davis (1975).

21. See Taylor et al. (1974:29–32); Davis (1975).

22. See Taylor et al. (1974:54).

23. Robinson (1999).

24. Taylor et al. (1974:31–32).

25. Taylor et al. (1974:35).

26. See Taylor et al. (1974:11, 19–21, 26, 32); Gouldner (1971); Davis (1975). Rafter (1997:239–240) claims that psychiatrists used the concept of psychopathy to wrest control of criminology from psychologists who then dominated the field and with whom psychiatrists were in competition. Laub and Sampson (1991:1404) attribute the heated debates about criminological theory between Edwin Sutherland and Bernard and Eleanor Glueck to "their respective methodological and disciplinary biases." Daly and Chesney-Lind (1988:500) maintain that "a major feminist project today is to expose the distortions and assumptions of androcentric science [which reveals] that an ideology of objectivity can serve to mask men's gender loyalties as well as loyalties to other class or racial groups." Cullen and others (1997:387) argue that Herrnstein and Murray's showing that IQ is a powerful predictor of crime in their controversial book *The Bell Curve*, and their resultant crime control policies, are based on the authors' ideology, "not on intelligent science." For a recent study showing that criminological theorizing is driven by sociopolitical ideology, see Walsh and Ellis (1999).

4

⊞

Biological Theories

Physiognomy

Phrenology

Criminal Anthropology

Body Type Theories

Heredity Studies

Modern Biocriminology

General Problems with Biological Theories

B iological theories of crime causation (*biological positivism*) are based on the belief that criminals are physiologically different from non-criminals. Early biological theories assumed that structure determines function.[1] In other words, criminals behave differently because structurally they are different.[2] Today's biocriminologists are more likely to assume that biochemistry determines function or, more precisely, the difference between criminals and noncriminals is the result of a complex interaction between biochemical and environmental factors (more about this later). To test biological theories, researchers try to demonstrate, through measurement and statistical analysis, that there are or are not significant structural or biochemical differences between criminals and noncriminals.[3]

Historically, the cause of crime, from this perspective, was *biological inferiority*. Biological inferiority in criminals was assumed to produce certain physical or genetic characteristics that distinguished criminals from noncriminals.[4] It is important to emphasize that the physical or genetic characteristics themselves did not cause crime, they were only the symptoms, or stigmata, of the more fundamental inferiority.[5] The concept of biological inferiority has lost favor among today's biocriminologists who generally prefer to emphasize the biological differences between criminals and noncriminals without adding the value judgment. In any event, several different methodologies have been employed to detect physical differences between criminals and noncriminals. They are physiognomy, phrenology, criminal anthropology, study of body types, heredity studies, including family trees, statistical comparisons, twin studies, and adoption studies; and, in the last ten to fifteen years or so, studies based on new scientific technologies that allow, for example, the examination of brain chemistry processes.

PHYSIOGNOMY

Physiognomy is the judging of character or disposition from facial and other physical features. The methodology has been attributed to the Swiss scholar and theologian Johan Caspar Lavater (1741–1781), who in 1775 published a four-volume work on the subject called *Physiognomical Fragments*.[6] The book, according to Vold and Bernard, was well received in Europe at the time and was nearly as popular as Beccaria's *On Crimes and Punishments*.[7]

The "science" of physiognomy has been traced to ancient Greece and Rome.[8] Curran and Renzetti note that during the Middle Ages, a law specified that when "two people were suspected of having committed the same crime, the uglier one should be regarded as more likely the guilty party."[9] However, by the middle of the eighteenth century, physiognomy had fallen into disrepute. As evidence, Curran and Renzetti cite a British law that "made all persons pretending to have skill in physiognomy liable to be whipped as rogues and vagabonds."[10] In any event, today the "science" of physiognomy primarily is of historical interest, as the precursor of the better-developed phrenology.[11]

PHRENOLOGY

Phrenology (or *craniology*) is the estimation of character and intelligence based on an examination of the shape of the skull (or cranium). Phrenology is associated with the work of Franz Joseph Gall (1758–1828) and his student and collaborator John Gaspar Spurzheim (1776–1832),[12] who are considered by some commentators as the fathers of criminology.[13]

The three basic propositions of phrenology are derived from Aristotle's belief that the brain is the organ of the mind:[14]

1. The exterior of the skull conforms to the interior and to the shape of the brain.
2. The "mind" consists of faculties or functions.
3. These faculties are related to the shape of the brain and skull; hence, just as the brain is the "organ of the mind," these "bumps" are indicators of the "organs" of the special faculties.

The faculties (for example, combativeness, friendliness, destructiveness, secretiveness, philoprogenitiveness—love of one's children) presumably are grouped into three regions, or compartments, of the mind: the active propensities, the moral sentiments, and the intellectual faculties.[15] The three regions are in equilibrium in the noncriminal, but in the criminal the active propensities are dominant.[16] It is interesting to note that the three regions of the mind are analogous to Freud's later formulation of the id, ego, and superego. Whether Freud was familiar with the earlier formulation is not known. In any event, phrenology was very popular during the first half of the nineteenth century and only lost its appeal because of its determinism, which was assailed as being antireligious and anti–free will.[17]

CRIMINAL ANTHROPOLOGY

Criminal anthropology is the study of "criminal" human beings. It is associated with the work of an Italian army doctor, and later university professor, Cesare Lombroso (1835–1909). Lombroso, who also is known as the father of criminology,[18] first published his theory of a physical criminal type in 1876. Although he had autopsied nearly four hundred prisoners and had taken precise measurements of various bodily organs of approximately six thousand additional prisoners and three thousand soldiers, according to Lombroso, his theory emerged as a revelation following his autopsy of a reputed bandit by the name of Vilella.[19] As Lombroso explained:

> This was not merely an idea, but a revelation. At the sight of that skull, I seemed to see all of a sudden, lighted up as a vast plain under a flaming sky, the problem of the nature of the criminal—an atavistic being who reproduces in his person the ferocious instincts of primitive humanity and the inferior animals. Thus were explained anatomically the enormous jaws, high cheek-bones, prominent superciliar arches, solitary lines in the palms, extreme size of the orbits, handle-shaped or sessile ears found in criminals, savages, and apes, insensitivity to pain, extremely acute sight, tattooing, excessive idleness, love of orgies, and the irresistible craving for evil for its own sake, the desire not only to extinguish life in the victim, but to mutilate the corpse, tear its flesh, and drink its blood.[20]

Lombroso's theory consisted of the following propositions:[21] First, criminals are, by birth, a distinct type. Second, that type can be recognized by stigmata or anomalies like those listed in the quote above. Third, the criminal type clearly is distinguished in a person with more than five stigmata, perhaps exists in a person with three to five stigmata, and does not necessarily exist in a person with less than three stigmata. Fourth, physical stigmata do not cause crime; they are only indicative of an individual who is predisposed to crime. Such a person is either an *atavist*—that is, a reversion to a savage type—or a result of degeneration. Fifth, because of their personal natures, such persons cannot desist from crime unless they experience very favorable lives.

In subsequent editions of his book, Lombroso described other causes of crime besides atavism. Crimes also were caused by insanity, epilepsy, passion (a cause of political crimes), poor parenting or education ("habitual criminals"), predispositions activated by particular environmental conditions or opportunities ("criminaloids"), and for reasons such as self-defense or the defense of family honor ("pseudocriminals").[22] In later editions of *The Criminal Man*, as well as in *Crime Its Causes and Remedies* (originally published in 1911), Lombroso paid considerable attention to social causes of crime. Lombroso's theory was popular in the United States until about 1915, although variations of his theory are still being presented today.

Two main problems with Lombroso's criminal anthropology are apparent. First is the assumption that certain physical characteristics indicate biological inferiority. Unless independent evidence supports that assumption, other than the association of the physical characteristics with criminality, then the result is circular reasoning.[23] In other words, crime is caused by biological inferiority, which is itself indicated by the physical characteristics associated with criminality.

A second problem is the assumption that apes and other lower animals are savage and criminal. As Gould remarks, "If some men look like apes, but apes be kind, then the argument fails."[24] In an effort to make the dubious connection, Lombroso had to engage in a tortured anthropomorphism. As Gould relates:

> He [Lombroso] cites, for example, an ant driven by rage to kill and dismember an aphid; an adulterous stork who, with her lover, murdered her husband; a criminal association of beavers who ganged up to murder a solitary compatriot; a male ant, without access to female reproductives, who violated a (female) worker with atrophied sexual organs, causing her great pain and death; he even refers to the insect eating of certain plants as an "equivalent of crime."[25]

Two of Lombroso's students—Enrico Ferri (1856–1928) and Raffaele Garofalo (1852–1934)—together with Lombroso have been called the Italian school of criminology. Though they differed somewhat in their analyses of crime, they were all positivists and opposed the freewill ontology of their fellow Italian Beccaria and the other classical thinkers. The subject of Ferri's dissertation was the problem of free will.[26]

Although Ferri emphasized biological causes of crime—he coined the term "born criminal"—he also believed that crime was the product of multiple factors, including physical factors (such as race, climate, and geography), anthropological factors (such as age, gender, and psychological attributes), and social factors (such as population density, religion, customs, organization of government, and economic conditions).[27] Consistent with his socialist beliefs, Ferri advocated the following crime prevention policies: free trade, abolition of monopolies, subsidized housing, public savings banks, better street lighting, birth control, freedom of marriage and divorce, state control of weapons manufacturing, foundling homes, and public recreation facilities.[28] Later in life he became a fascist and, in the 1920s, was invited by Mussolini to draft a new penal code for Italy.[29] His penal code, which reflected his positivist and socialist/fascist beliefs, was rejected for departing too much from classical legal thought.[30]

Garofalo, on the other hand, rejected Ferri's belief in environmental causes of crime as well as Lombroso's theory of atavism. Instead, Garofalo, adopting principles of Social Darwinism, believed that crime was a natural product of adaptation; criminals were physically unable to adapt to society. Therefore, argued Garofalo, most criminals were unfit

to survive and should be eliminated from society through extermina-
tion in the case of criminals who committed serious offenses or long-
term imprisonment, life imprisonment, or overseas transportation for
criminals who committed lesser offenses. For criminals who committed
crimes under exceptional circumstances and who were not likely to
repeat them, Garofalo advocated "enforced reparation."[31] It should not
be surprising that Garofalo's ideas, like those of Ferri, were popular during Mussolini's fascist regime in Italy. This underscores a potential problem with positivist theories: They can easily be used to justify, on a
scientific basis, ideas that promote racial purity, national power, and
authoritarian leadership.[32]

BODY TYPE THEORIES

Body type theories are an extension of Lombroso's criminal anthropology. William Sheldon (1898–1977), whose work in the 1940s was
based on earlier work by Ernst Kretchmer in the 1920s, is perhaps the
best known of the body type theorists. According to Sheldon, human
beings can be divided into three basic body types, or *somatotypes*,
which correspond to three basic temperaments:[33] the endomorphic
(soft, fat), the mesomorphic (athletically built, muscular), and the ecto-
morphic (thin, delicate).

Sheldon argued that everyone has elements of all three types but that
one type usually predominates. In a study of two hundred Boston
delinquents between 1939 and 1949, Sheldon found that delinquents
were more mesomorphic than nondelinquents and that serious delinquents were more mesomorphic than less serious delinquents.[34]
Subsequent studies by the Gluecks in the 1950s and by Cortes in the
1970s also found the association between mesomorphy and delinquency.[35] The studies by Cortes, moreover, used more precise measurement techniques than those by either Sheldon or the Gluecks, who
were criticized on this account.

The major criticism of the body type theories is that differences in
behavior reflect the social selection process and not biological inferiority.[36] In other words, delinquents are more likely to be mesomorphic
than nondelinquents because, for example, mesomorphs are more likely
to be selected for gang membership. Additionally, the finding that delinquents are more likely than nondelinquents to be mesomorphic contra-
dicts the general assumption that criminals (or delinquents) are
biologically inferior, at least with regard to physique.

In any event, if one assumes that crime is the product of biological inferiority, then the crime prevention implications are rather

straightforward. You either isolate criminals, sterilize them, exterminate them, or employ some combination of the three.

HEREDITY STUDIES

A variety of methods have been employed to test the proposition that
criminals are genetically different from noncriminals. Perhaps the earliest methodology was the use of family trees. Usually a family known
to have many "criminals" was compared with an exemplary family.
This was the technique used by Dugdale and by Estabrook, who both
compared the Jukes family with the Edwards family.[37] The Jukes family presumably had seven murderers, sixty thieves, fifty prostitutes, and
assorted other criminals. The Edwards family, on the other hand, presumably had no criminals but, instead, had presidents of the United
States, governors, Supreme Court and federal court judges, and
assorted writers, preachers, and teachers. As it turns out, the Edwards
family was not as exemplary as originally believed. Apparently,
Jonathan Edwards's maternal grandmother had been divorced on
grounds of adultery, a grandaunt had murdered her son, and a
granduncle had murdered his sister.

Be that as it may, a finding that criminality appears in successive
generations does not prove that criminality is inherited or is the product of a hereditary defect. For example, the use of a fork in eating has
been a trait of many families for many generations, but that does not
prove that the use of a fork is inherited. In short, the family tree
method cannot adequately separate hereditary influences from environmental influences.[38]

A second methodology used to test the proposition that crime is
inherited or is the product of a hereditary defect is statistical compari-
son. Charles Goring (1870–1919) was perhaps the first social scientist to
argue that if criminality exhibited the same degree of family resemblance as other physical traits, such as eye or hair color, then criminality, like those other traits, must be inherited.[39] In tests of his theory,
Goring indeed found that associations between general criminality, as
measured by imprisonment, and parental and fraternal resemblance for
ordinary physical traits, as well as for inherited defects such as insanity,
were remarkably similar.

Goring was not naive, however, and recognized that the associations
that he found might be the result of environmental factors rather than,
or in addition to, genetic factors. Thus, in separate analyses he
attempted to determine the influence of environmental factors. A

problem was that he only considered eight environmental factors. A more telling criticism of Goring's findings is that he limited his study to male offenders, although he notes that the ratio of brothers to sisters in prison is seventeen to one. If criminality is inherited in the same way that hair or eye color is, then one would expect it to affect females to relatively the same extent as it does males unless, of course, criminality is a sex-linked trait. In short, statistical comparisons cannot adequately separate hereditary influences from environmental influences.

A third, more sophisticated method of testing the proposition that crime is inherited or is the result of a hereditary defect is the use of twin studies.[40] Heredity is assumed to be the same in identical twins because they are the product of a single egg. Heredity is assumed to be different in fraternal twins because they are the product of two eggs fertilized by two sperm. The logic of the method is that if there is greater similarity in behavior between identical twins than between fraternal twins, then the behavior must be due to heredity, since environments are much the same. More than a half century of using this methodology reveals that identical twins are more likely to demonstrate concordance (where both twins have criminal records) than are fraternal twins, thus supporting the hereditary link.

A problem with the twin studies, however, is the potential confounding of genetic and environmental influences. Identical twins tend to be treated more alike by others, spend much more time together, and share a greater sense of mutual identity than do fraternal twins.[41] For nine months they also shared a critical environment inside the same mother.[42] All those factors are important environmental influences, and, when environmental influences are controlled, studies show that the difference in criminality between identical and fraternal twins is not significant.[43]

A fourth method, and the most recent and sophisticated way of examining the inheritability of criminality, is the adoption study.[44] The first such study was conducted in the 1970s. In this method, the criminal records of adopted children (almost always boys) who are adopted at a relatively early age are compared with the criminal records of both their biological parents and their adoptive parents (almost always fathers). The rationale is that if the criminal records of adopted boys are more like those of their biological fathers than like those of their adoptive fathers, the criminality of the adopted boys can be assumed to be the result of heredity.

Findings of the adoption studies reveal that the percentage of adoptees who are criminal is greater when the biological father has a criminal record than when the adoptive father has one. However, there also is an interactive effect. In other words, a greater percentage of adoptees have criminal records when both fathers have criminal records than when only one of them does. Thus, like the twin studies, the adoption studies presumably demonstrate the influence of heredity but cannot adequately separate it from the influence of the environment. A problem with the adoption studies is the difficulty of interpreting the relative influences of heredity and environment, especially when the adoption does not take place shortly after birth or when, as is commonly the case, the adoption agency attempts to find an adoptive home that matches the biological home in family income and socioeconomic status.[45] In sum, a recent analysis of more than sixty years of research using studies of families, twins, and adoptees found that claims of a genetic link to criminality are based on very weak statistical evidence; indeed, the more methodologically sound the study, the weaker the relationship found.[46]

MODERN BIOCRIMINOLOGY

Ongoing research has revealed numerous biological factors associated either directly or indirectly with criminal or delinquent behavior. Among such factors are certain chemical, mineral, and vitamin deficiencies in the diet, diets high in sugar and carbohydrates, hypoglycemia (low blood sugar level), certain allergies, ingestion of food dyes and lead, exposure to radiation from fluorescent tubes and television sets, and all sorts of brain dysfunctions such as attention deficit/hyperactivity disorder.[47] This section focuses on a few more of the biological factors linked to criminality and delinquency: disorders of the limbic system and other parts of the brain, brain chemical dysfunctions, minimal brain damage, endocrine abnormalities, and undetected hearing loss.

At least some unprovoked violent criminal behavior is believed to be caused by tumors and other destructive or inflammatory processes of the limbic system.[48] Psychopaths (discussed in the next chapter on psychological theories) are also believed to suffer from limbic system disorders.[49] The *limbic system* is a structure surrounding the brain stem and is the source of feelings of pleasure and pain.[50] It also controls, in part, the life functions of heartbeat, breathing, and sleep and is believed to moderate expressions of violence; such emotions as anger, rage, and fear; and sexual response.[51] Violent criminal behavior has also been linked to disorders in other parts of the brain.[52] Recent evidence suggests that chronic violent offenders have much higher levels of brain disorder when compared to the general population.[53]

The destructive processes of the limbic system and other brain disorders sometimes can be recognized by abnormal EEGs (electroencephalograms), PET (positron emission tomography) scans, or MRIs (magnetic resonance imaging),[54] and surgical removal of the affected area sometimes eliminates expressions of violence.[55] Problems with that type of intervention, however, are that it can cause unpredictable and undesirable behavior changes, and, of course, it is irreversible.[56] Irreversibility is less a problem with newer chemical interventions, but the problem of unpredictable and undesirable behavior changes remains.

Low levels of the brain neurotransmitter *serotonin* (a substance brain cells use to communicate) have been found in impulsive murderers and arsonists, and research is currently being conducted to determine whether low levels of the neurotransmitter *norepinephrine* are associated with compulsive gambling.[57] Another interesting finding in this area may help explain cocaine use. Apparently, cocaine increases the level of the neurotransmitter *dopamine*, which activates the limbic system to produce pleasure.[58] If such chemical dysfunctions are linked to those behaviors, chemical treatment or improved diets might help.[59]

Research on minimal brain damage has found that it is related to learning disabilities and increases an individual's chances of being identified as delinquent by contributing to poor school performance or dropping out of school.[60] Minimal brain damage is believed to be most commonly caused by nutritional or oxygen deficiencies in utero, or during or shortly after birth, or by insufficient protein and sensory stimulation during a child's formative years.[61] Because minimal brain damage also is strongly associated with lower socioeconomic status, social deprivation must be considered a critical element in its occurrence.[62]

To reduce minimal brain damage in the population, adequate prenatal medical care and nutrition would need to be provided to all expectant mothers to ensure that the uterine environment is supportive of the developing fetus.[63] To minimize perinatal complications, adequate medical assistance must be provided during birth.[64] Finally, minimal brain damage can be reduced by providing adequate protein diets and social and intellectual stimulation to developing infants and young children.[65]

Criminal behaviors also have been associated with endocrine abnormalities, especially those involving *testosterone* (the male sex hormone) and *progesterone* and *estrogen* (the female sex hormones).[66] For example, the administration of estrogen to male sex offenders has been found to reduce their sexual drives.[67] A similar effect has been achieved by administering the drug Depo Provera, which reduces testosterone levels.[68] However, a problem with Depo Provera is that it is only successful with those male sex offenders who cannot control their sexual urges. It does not seem to work on offenders whose sex crimes are premeditated.[69] A decline in the level of testosterone, which occurs naturally as people grow older, has also been used to explain why older people engage in violent behavior less frequently than do younger people.[70] Studies also have found a large percentage of female crimes committed during the menstrual or premenstrual periods of the female hormonal cycle. Those periods are characterized by an imbalance in the estrogen-progesterone ratio.[71]

At least four studies have found that between 17 and 48.5 percent of the incarcerated offenders examined have hearing losses.[72] The percentage of the general population with a hearing loss is about 7 percent. The difference suggests to the researchers that criminality may be linked to undetected hearing loss. The statistics are even more impressive when one considers that the 7 percent figure is for the entire population, whereas the larger figures are for the prison population, which has an average age of about twenty-five. One would expect a lower level of hearing loss among the younger prison population. As in many studies of this type, how a hearing loss might influence criminal behavior is not clear yet, but there is little question that much of the influence is through environmental factors.

GENERAL PROBLEMS
WITH BIOLOGICAL THEORIES

In the preceding sections, the different biological perspectives and the methodologies of each one have been described. Problems peculiar to a particular perspective or methodology also have been identified. In this section, some of the general problems with nearly all biological theories are presented.

One of the problems with biological theories of crime causation is that their crime prevention implications are so unsavory for many people. For most of the theories, besides those for which specific crime prevention implications already have been identified, the choice is to exterminate, isolate, or sterilize offenders. Despite their distastefulness for some, at one time or another, each of the penalties has been imposed. Regarding sterilization, between 1911 and 1930 in the United States, as part of the eugenics movement, at least sixty-four thousand people were legally sterilized for their "criminality, alcoholism, sodomy, bestiality, feeble-mindedness, and tendency to commit rape."[73] Sterilization continued to be used in the United States well into the 1970s in such states as Virginia and California.[74] Today, chemical castration is legal in at least four states—California, Florida, Georgia, and Texas.[75]

A second problem is that most of the biologically oriented research is methodologically poor.[76] For example, generalizations are made from small samples, subjects are not randomly selected or assigned, and there are either no control groups or inadequate ones. This is less true of more recent research, however.

Third, most of the subjects of this research are incarcerated at the time of study, which creates generalization problems.[77] Incarcerated offenders are not representative of all offenders (only those who have been caught, convicted, and imprisoned). Nor do prisoners include all people who have the biological trait in question, which makes it is impossible to determine whether prisoners are overrepresented with regard to the trait. With only prisoners as subjects, it is impossible to determine whether any observed effect (such as criminality) is due to the trait in question or to the experiences of confinement.

Fourth, the biology of an individual only provides a behavioral potential, not a realization.[78] Many people possess the physical characteristics associated with criminality but do not engage in crime, and many people who lack the physical characteristics associated with criminality do commit crime. Besides, the overall behavioral uniformities that exist in every society, given genetic diversity, suggests the primary influence of the environment on behavior.[79]

Fifth, "no behavior is per se criminal."[80] The relationship between biology and crime involves the interaction of biology and environment within the context of legislatively proscribed behavior.[81] The problem is that biological positivists rarely question the criminalization process. That is, they rarely consider why some behaviors are defined as criminal, whereas other similar behaviors are not.

Finally, very little of the "crime problem" can be considered to be related primarily to biological factors.[82] Obviously, the dramatic increase in the volume and severity of crime during the last two decades or so (until recently, according to government statistics) has not been accompanied by an equally dramatic shift in the biological composition of the population.[83] Nor, for that matter, can biological factors easily account for the great variation in crime rates across geographic areas (for example, cities, states, nations). People of different geographic areas are not that different biologically.

In sum, there probably are no positivist criminologists today who would argue that a biological or genetic imperative for crime exists. Nor, for that matter, are there many criminologists today, of any ideological persuasion, who would deny that biology has some influence on criminal behavior. Thus, the position held by most criminologists today is that criminal behavior is the product of a complex interaction between biology and environmental or social conditions.[84] What is inherited is not criminal behavior, but rather the way in which the person responds to the environment.[85] In short, biology or genetics provides an individual with a predisposition or a tendency to behave in a certain way.[86] Whether a person actualizes that predisposition or tendency and whether the subsequent behavior is defined as crime depend primarily on environmental or social conditions.

STUDY QUESTIONS

1. What is the cause of crime according to biological theories?

2. What is the perspective on which biological theories of crime causation are based?

3. What methodologies have been used to test the perspective on which biological theories of crime causation are based? (Describe them.)

4. What are some other, newer areas of biological research into crime causation?

5. How would biological positivists prevent crime?

6. What are general problems with biological theories of crime causation?

7. How do biological theories of crime causation compare to classical and neoclassical theories?

NOTES

1. Vold (1979:51). Structure and function probably are reciprocally related to each other. That is, not only does structure determine function but function also determines structure.

2. See Vold and Bernard (1986:84).

3. Vold (1979:51).

4. See Vold and Bernard (1986:47).

5. Vold (1979:52).

6. Vold and Bernard (1986:48). The theory has also been attributed to the sixteenth-century physiognomist J. Baptiste della Porte (see Williams and McShane, 1994:32).

7. Vold and Bernard (1986:48).

8. Curran and Renzetti (1994:39); Vold and Bernard (1986:47–48).

9. Curran and Renzetti (1994:39).

10. Curran and Renzetti (1994:39–40).

11. Vold and Bernard (1986:48).

12. Vold and Bernard (1986:48–49).

13. See Martin et al. (1990:24).

14. Vold and Bernard (1986:48).

15. Vold and Bernard (1986:49).

16. Vold and Bernard (1986:49).

17. Vold and Bernard (1986:49–50).

18. See Williams and McShane (1994:33).

19. Taylor et al. (1974:41).

20. Cited in Taylor et al. (1974:41).

21. See Vold and Bernard (1986:50–51); also see Lombroso (1968:xxii, xxiv, xxv).

22. Curran and Renzetti (1994:43); also see Lombroso (1968). Lombroso estimated that about 40 percent of criminals were atavists (Lombroso 1968:xxx).

23. See Vold and Bernard (1986:57).

24. Gould (1981:125).

25. Gould (1981:125).

26. Lanier and Henry (1998:93).

27. Lanier and Henry (1998:94–95); Lilly et al. (1989:30); Vold and Bernard (1986:41).

28. Lilly et al. (1989:30); Vold and Bernard (1986:41).

29. Lilley et al. (1989:30–31).

30. Lilly et al. (1989:31).

31. Lanier and Henry (1998:96); Lilly et al. (1989:32–34); Vold and Bernard (1986:44).

32. Lilly et al. (1989:34–35); Vold and Bernard (1986:42).

33. Sheldon (1949).

34. See Vold and Bernard (1986:60).

35. Glueck and Glueck (1956); Cortes (1972).

36. See Curran and Renzetti (1994:53); Vold and Bernard (1986:63).

37. Dugdale (1877); Estabrook (1916).

38. Fishbein (1990:44).

39. Goring (1913); also see Vold and Bernard (1986:52–55).

40. See Wilson and Herrnstein (1985:90–95); Vold and Bernard (1986:87–90).

41. Curran and Renzetti (1994:59); Fishbein (1990:44–45).

42. Morris (1998:324).

43. See, for example, Dalgard and Kringlen (1976); but also see Fishbein (1990:44) for a different view.

44. See Wilson and Herrnstein (1985:95–100); Vold and Bernard (1986:90–92).

45. See Vold and Bernard (1986:92); Fishbein (1990:45–46).

46. Walters (1992).

47. See, for example, Fishbein (2000).

48. Shah and Roth (1974); Mark and Ervin (1970).

49. Fishbein (1990:38).

50. Fishbein (1990:37).

51. Mark and Ervin (1970).

52. Raine et al. (1997).

53. Pallone and Hennessy (1998).

54. National Institute (1977:119); also see Fishbein and Thatcher (1986).

55. National Institute (1977:127–128); Mark and Ervin (1970).

56. National Institute (1977:128).

57. Curran and Renzetti (1994:78): also see Fishbein (1990:47); Ellis and Walsh (1997:259).

58. Fishbein (1990:38).

59. Neurotransmitters are products of the foods people eat.

60. National Institute (1977:120–122); Shah and Roth (1974); Vold and Bernard (1986:101–103).

61. National Institute (1977:120–121).

62. National Institute (1977:128).

63. National Institute (1977:129).

64. National Institute (1977:129).

65. National Institute (1977:129).

66. National Institute (1977); Shah and Roth (1974); Fishbein (1990:48).

67. See Wilson and Herrnstein (1985:120); National Institute (1977:119, 128).

68. Fishbein (1990:53); Andrews and Bonta (1994:225).

69. Curran and Renzetti (1994:80–81).

70. Gove (1985); also see Fishbein (1990:48).

71. See Wilson and Herrnstein (1985:121); Curran and Renzetti (1994:73–77); Vold and Bernard (1986:97–98); Fishbein (1990:48).

72. "Footnotes" (1987:A6); Eyre (1988:13A).

73. Lilly et al. (1989:43).

74. Lilly et al. (1989:44).

75. Bohm and Haley (1999:75).

76. National Institute (1977:127); Walters and White (1989); Fishbein (1990:39–40).

77. See Taylor et al. (1974:44, 285, fn. 7); Walters and White (1989:478); Fishbein (1990:39).

78. National Institute (1977:110).

79. National Institute (1977:110).

80. National Institute (1977:111).

81. National Institute (1977:111); Fishbein (1990).

82. National Institute (1977:111).

83. National Institute (1977:111); Taylor et al. (1974:43).

84. See Wilson and Herrnstein (1985:70); Fishbein (1990:41).

85. Fishbein (1990:42).

86. Fishbein (1990:42); Ellis and Walsh (1997:229–230).

5

Psychological Theories

Intelligence and Crime

Psychoanalytic Theories

General Problems with Psychoanalytic Theories

Humanistic Psychological Theory

I n this chapter, psychological theories of crime causation (*psychological positivism*) are examined. The chapter begins with a description of the relationship between intelligence and criminality and delinquency and proceeds to discussions of psychoanalytic and humanistic psychological theories. Learning or behavioral theories are reserved for the section on the modifications to Sutherland's differential association theory in Chapter 6.

INTELLIGENCE AND CRIME

The idea that crime is the product primarily of people of low intelligence was popular in the United States between 1914 and about 1930. It received some attention again during the mid-1970s and experienced a modest revival in the mid-1990s, beginning with the publication of

Richard Herrnstein (1930–1994) and Charles Murray's (1943–) *The Bell Curve* in 1994. The belief requires only a slight shift in thinking from the idea that criminals are biologically inferior to the idea that they are mentally inferior.

One of the earliest promoters in the United States of the relationship between low IQ and crime was H. H. Goddard (1866–1957). In 1914 he published *Feeblemindedness: Its Causes and Consequences*. In the book, Goddard argued that criminals are *feebleminded*, an old-fashioned term that has been replaced by the more modern *mentally retarded* or *mentally challenged* (of below-normal intelligence).

To test his proposition, Goddard first had to determine what IQ level constituted feeblemindedness, so he administered IQ tests to all inmates of the New Jersey Training School for the Feeble Minded at Vineland where he worked. He discovered that none of the tested residents had a mental age over thirteen and therefore concluded that a mental age of twelve (which is equivalent to an IQ of 75) was the upper-threshold level of feeblemindedness.[1] At the time, Goddard believed that an IQ above 75 was normal. Today, however, 90 to 110 is considered the normal range for IQ.

In any event, armed with a standard for feeblemindedness, Goddard and many other psychologists began testing a variety of different populations, including prison and jail inmates. The proportion of subjects in those studies determined to be feebleminded varied greatly from a low of 28 percent to a high of 89 percent.[2] The studies of prisoners, however, revealed that 70 percent had IQs of 75 or less which, for Goddard, provided strong support for his proposition.[3]

A problem arose when the Army Psychological Corps adopted Goddard's standard as a criterion for fitness for military service. When intelligence tests were administered to draftees for World War I, it was discovered that about one-third of them were feebleminded using Goddard's criterion.[4] Whether that was an accurate indicator of the intelligence level of the population at the time (as represented by the draft army) must remain the object of conjecture. However, as a practical matter, the army was not about to eliminate nearly one-third of draftees because of low-level intelligence. Consequently, Goddard changed his conclusions. In 1927, he wrote:

> The war led to the measurement of intelligence of the drafted
> army with the result that such an enormous proportion was found
> to have an intelligence of 12 years and less that to call them all fee-
> ble minded was an absurdity of the highest degree. . . . We have
> already said that we thought 12 was the limit, but we now know

that most of the twelve, and even of the ten [IQ = 63] and nine [IQ = 56], are not defective.[5]

In 1931 Sutherland reviewed approximately 350 studies on the relationship between intelligence and delinquency and criminality.[6] The studies reported the results of intelligence tests of about 175,000 criminals and delinquents. Sutherland concluded from the review that although intelligence may play a role in individual cases, given the selection that takes place in arrest, conviction, and imprisonment, the distribution of the intelligence scores of criminals and delinquents is very similar to the distribution of the intelligence scores of the general population.

For the next forty years or so, the issue regarding the relationship between intelligence and crime and delinquency appeared resolved. However, in the mid-1970s, two studies were published that resurrected the debate, one by Gordon in 1976 and the other by Hirschi and Hindelang in 1977.[7] These studies found that IQ was an important predictor of both official and self-reported delinquency, as important as social class or race.[8] Hirschi and Hindelang acknowledged the findings of Sutherland's earlier review, noting that a decreasing number of delinquents had been reported as feebleminded over the years but that the difference in intelligence between delinquents and nondelinquents had never disappeared and had stabilized at about eight IQ points.[9] They failed to note, however, that the eight-point IQ difference generally was within the normal range. Hirschi and Hindelang surmised that IQ influenced delinquency through its effect on school performance.[10]

In the mid-to-late 1990s, a series of books were published claiming that intelligence or IQ was primarily the product of genetics, and that genetic differences in intelligence could, in large measure, explain racial differences in crime. Specifically, the theory is that genetic differences in intelligence are the principal reason why Blacks commit a disproportionately high percentage of violent crime and "all categories of felony except those requiring access to large amounts of money, such as stock fraud."[11] In addition to Herrnstein and Murray's *The Bell Curve* (1994), other books in this genre include J. Philippe Rushton's *Race, Evolution, and Behavior* (1995), Michael Levin's *Why Race Matters* (1997), and Arthur Jensen's *The g Factor* (1998).[12] The following description of their theory could easily have been placed in the previous chapter on biological theories, because it is unquestionably biological. However, because of the theory's focus on IQ as the key explanatory factor, the theory is more accurately called evolutionary biopsychological.[13]

The theory proposes that IQ, in large measure, determines a person's ability to control or restrain his or her impulses. It assumes that most "street crime" is caused by people unable to control their impulses.[14] Put differently, the theory posits a positive relationship between IQ and impulse control, and a negative relationship between impulse control and crime. The theorists cite a large body of evidence showing significant mean or average differences in IQ among races, with Orientals, on average, having the highest IQs, Blacks, on average, having the lowest IQs, and Whites having IQs that, on average, fall between those of Orientals and Blacks. These IQ differences among the races, according to the theory, are mostly, but not exclusively, genetic-evolutionary in origin.

Evolutionary biologists generally believe that modern humans evolved in Africa about 200,000 years ago, and that some Africans began migrating out of Africa about 110,000 years ago. The further north people migrated out of Africa, the more they encountered different climates and geographies that required different skills and lifestyles. The different climates also necessitated differences in skin pigmentation and other physical characteristics and, thus, different races—Whites and Orientals—evolved. Orientals and Whites presumably split about 40,000 years ago. Because intelligence increased the chances of survival in harsh winter climates, unknown to those in Africa, the migrants had to evolve greater intelligence and lifestyle changes—hence the greater average intelligence level of Orientals and Whites compared to Blacks. In sum, the theory holds that climatic and geographical changes genetically altered human beings into different races distinguishable, in part, by average intelligence. Intelligence largely determines impulse-control ability, which, in turn, determines the likelihood of crime.

A corollary of the theory is that less intelligent Blacks are less responsible for their crimes and lives in general because they have less impulse control.[15] This assumption and the race-IQ-crime theory from which it is derived have been used to justify the following policies to reduce crimes by Blacks. First, welfare, especially Aid to Families with Dependent Children, must be eliminated because it has made "reckless" black behavior "cost-free." Second, many civil rights won by Blacks, as well as expanded black social mobility, the application of the same rules to both Black and White offenders, and the general reduction in criminal penalties imposed on Blacks, all must be eliminated. Proponents of the theory argue that it is no coincidence that during the past three decades the aforementioned social changes were accompanied by an increase in black crime. Third, race-based penalties must be established if rewards for good behavior prove ineffective because people with less self-control (disproportionately Blacks) require harsher penalties to deter them from crime. Fourth, certain well-intentioned crime control strategies, such as community centers and midnight basketball leagues, must be eliminated because they condone and reward violent criminal behavior. The same is true of prison educational, vocational, and recreational programs. Fifth, because of differences in physical maturation rates—Blacks, on average, mature physically earlier than Whites, on average—Black offenders should be treated as adults at an earlier age. Sixth, because Blacks, on average, exercise less self-control than other races and, therefore, are more difficult to deter, they should receive swifter punishment and stricter limits on appeals. Seventh, there should be greater surveillance of young Black males by the police.

In addition to being subject to criticisms about the meanings of IQ and race in general,[16] this race-IQ-crime theory is a biological theory and, therefore, subject to many of the same criticisms of biological theories described in the last chapter. For instance, the theory overpredicts and does not explain exceptions well. Most Blacks with low IQs do not commit violent crimes and other felonies, and Blacks with high IQs do commit such crimes. Additionally, preliminary findings from the Human Genome Diversity Project—the first worldwide survey of humankind—suggest that the racial differences assumed by the theory's proponents may be overstated. The Project's analysis of thousands of DNA samples reveals the "generic unity that binds our diverse, polyglot species." The data show that "any two people, regardless of geography or ethnicity, share at least 99.99 percent of their genetic makeup." As for the 0.01 percent of the genome that makes people different, "it doesn't shake out along racial lines. . . Instead, some 85 percent of human genetic diversity occurs within ethnic groups, not between them."[17] The policy implications of the theory that were listed earlier also seem harsh, mean-spirited, and racist.

As for intelligence and crime, race notwithstanding, the conclusion cannot be drawn with any degree of confidence that delinquents, as a group, are less intelligent than nondelinquents.[18] Most adult criminals are not feebleminded.[19] Obviously, low-level intelligence cannot account for gender differences in crime or the dramatic increase in the crime rate over the last couple of decades (until recently, according to government statistics), unless, in the latter case, one is prepared to assume that the population of offenders is getting less intelligent or is growing.[20] Since IQs do not increase with age, why do most criminal offenders stop committing crimes as they get older? Low-level intelligence certainly cannot account for complex white-collar and political crimes.[21]

PSYCHOANALYTIC THEORIES

Psychoanalytic theories of crime causation are associated with the work of Sigmund Freud (1859–1939) and his followers.[22] Freud did not theorize much about criminal behavior per se, but a theory of crime causation can be inferred from his more general theory of human behavior and its disorders. Had he contemplated the issue, Freud probably would have argued that crime, like other disorders, was a symptom of more deep-seated problems. Considered here are four deep-seated problems of which crime might be considered symptomatic by Freud: (1) difficulties or problems during one of the psychosexual stages of development, (2) an inability to sublimate (or redirect) sexual and aggressive drives, (3) an inability to successfully resolve (as to settle a problem) the Oedipal (in men) or Electra (in women) complex, and (4) an unconscious desire for punishment.

According to Freud, five normal, universal stages characterize human *psychosexual development*: (1) the oral stage, (2) the anal stage, (3) the phallic stage, (4) the latency stage, and (5) the genital stage. Crime has been considered by some psychoanalytic positivists as symptomatic of problems during four of the stages. The problems are either a *fixation* (arrested development) at a particular stage or a *regression* (a return) to an earlier one.

The *oral stage* of psychosexual development (from birth to around one year old) is the period of breast-feeding, and alcoholism and drug addiction have been considered symptomatic of problems during this stage. Presumably alcohol and drugs satisfy the need for infantile oral pleasure.

The *anal stage* is the toilet-training period (from one through three years old), and embezzlement and armed robbery have been attributed to problems in this stage. The embezzler or robber unconsciously "holds on to" or "will not let go of" the symbol for excrement (the stolen goods).

Problems during the *phallic stage* (around three to six years of age), during which the child begins to understand the pleasure that can be had from his or her sexual organs, have been associated with an excessive interest in sex resulting, in extreme cases, in sexual assault, rape, or prostitution—the result of unresolved Oedipal or Electra conflicts (to be discussed shortly).[23] Unresolved Oedipal or Electra conflicts have also been used to explain sexual promiscuity, hostility toward male authority figures, and running away.[24]

No references could be found that associated any criminal behaviors with the *latency stage* (from about six years of age to puberty), during which the sex drive seems to disappear (it is repressed).

Finally, prostitution and homosexuality (which is not a crime, although in some states certain homosexual acts are) have been considered symptomatic of problems with sexual identity during the *genital stage*, which begins with the onset of puberty.

A second deep-seated problem of which crime has been considered symptomatic is the inability to sublimate sexual and aggressive drives. For Freud, all human beings are born with those two drives; they are the primary sources of human motivation. Ideally, people are able to *sublimate* (redirect) sexual and aggressive drives either to legal nonsexual or nonaggressive outlets or to legal sexual and aggressive outlets. Examples of the former are reading and hobbies of various sorts; examples of the latter are marriage and contact sports. If unsuccessful at sublimating the drives, they will be either acted out (perhaps as violent criminal behavior) or *repressed* (rendered unconscious). *Unconscious* refers to mental processes of which the person is unaware. If the drives are repressed, they may be acted out anytime in later life, again possibly as criminal behavior. The acting out of repressed sexual and aggressive drives might explain the supposedly inexplicable crime, as when the angelic, church-going, Eagle Scout kills, dismembers, and cannibalizes a victim. Repressed sexual and aggressive drives, if not acted out, can lead to mental conflict that manifests itself in *anxiety* (distress or worry). To keep anxiety under control and to maintain psychic equilibrium, *defense mechanisms* are employed.

Freud identified a variety of defense mechanisms. Among them are *perceptual vigilance* (seeing only what you want to see), *perceptual defense* (blocking out what you do not want to see), *repression* (forcing ideas out of consciousness), *rationalization* (intentionally misperceiving or redefining a situation), *introjection* (internalizing external objects and making them a part of your personality), and *projection* (interpreting situations based on internal states or emotions).

In 1957, Gresham Sykes (1922–) and David Matza (1930–) published an influential study entitled "Techniques of Neutralization: A Theory of Delinquency," in which they used Freud's defense mechanisms (they called them "techniques of neutralization") to explain delinquent behavior.[25] According to Sykes and Matza, "Much delinquency is based on what is essentially an unrecognized extension of defenses to crimes, in the form of justifications [or rationalizations] for deviance that are seen as valid by the delinquent but not by the legal system or society at large."[26] Sykes and Matza described five techniques of neutralization: (1) *denial of responsibility* ("I didn't mean to do it" or "I'm sick"), (2) *denial of injury* ("Nobody got hurt"), (3) *denial of victim* ("They had it coming to them" or "We weren't hurting anyone"), (4) *condemnation of the condemners* ("Everybody does it"), and (5) *appeal to higher loyalties* ("I only did it for the gang"). For Sykes and Matza, it is by learning those defenses that the juvenile becomes delinquent, rather than by learning laws, values, or attitudes. Most delinquents, according to Sykes and Matza, believe in the dominant value system of society. Indeed, if asked, most delinquents would readily admit that their delinquent activities are wrong. Consequently, if delinquents could not justify their delinquent behavior and thus reduce the guilt they would feel otherwise, they would not engage in it.[27] Note that Sykes and Matza's neutralizations are made prior to a delinquent act—to free an individual of guilt to commit it—while Freud's defense mechanisms are generally employed after a delinquent act to reduce guilt (and anxiety) caused by it.

A policy implication of neutralization theory would be to delegitimate neutralizations, that is, make them unacceptable. One way that might be accomplished is by reducing or eliminating social injustices and double standards. Such a strategy would require formidable structural changes.

A problem with Sykes and Matza's neutralization theory involves the degree to which juvenile offenders, and people generally, are committed to conventional values and norms. If they are not committed— a presumption of many social control theories—neutralization is unnecessary.[28] Matza (1964) later conceded that few people (juveniles or adults) are *always* committed to conventional values and norms, but, instead, that most people typically *drift* between law-abiding and law-violating behaviors. Whether or not they commit crime depends largely on opportunity. Another question about neutralization theory is whether neutralizations occur before or after delinquent acts. Research suggests that they occur both before and after such acts.[29] Finally, the theory fails to explain how neutralizations originate or who invented them.[30]

A third deep-seated problem of which crime has been considered symptomatic is the inability to successfully resolve the Oedipal (in men) or Electra (in women) complex. This inability explains why an individual fails to develop a strong superego. For Freud, the superego, together with the id and the ego, are the three parts of the mind. The *superego* is the conscience or source of morality and is mainly unconscious. Its functions include (1) approval or disapproval of the ego's actions, that is, judgment that an act is "right" or "wrong"; (2) critical self-observation; (3) self-punishment; and (4) self-love or self-esteem. The *id* is the energy system of the mind (*libido*); it is the source of the instinctive sexual and aggressive drives. The id resides in the unconscious and is governed by the *pleasure principle*; in other words, it only seeks pleasure. The id is controlled by the ego and superego. The *ego* is the part of the mind that mediates between the individual and reality. It is governed by the *reality principle*. Its prime function is the perception of reality and adaptation to it so as to maximize pleasure and minimize pain. The ego does not judge right from wrong or good from bad, which is the job of the superego.

Although concern here is with superego problems, it is important to note that criminality has also been attributed to a weak ego. An individual with a weak ego is characterized by "immaturity, poorly developed social skills, poor reality testing, gullibility and excessive dependence."[31] Such an individual may stumble into trouble because of a misreading of the external environment, temper tantrums, or following the lead of someone else.[32]

Returning to the *Oedipal* and *Electra complexes*, between the ages of three and six (during the phallic stage of psychosexual development), the child develops a monopoly feeling for the opposite-sexed parent. For Freud, this is a normal, universal process. At this age (during which the ego already has developed), the child realizes that the like-sexed parent will get mad if the other parent directs all of his or her attention to the child. The male child (we will return to the female child shortly) becomes afraid that his father will castrate him if this occurs. Because of a fear of castration, the little boy represses his desire for his mother and overreacts and identifies with his father. Presumably, the repressed desire for the mother manifests itself in little boys at this age frequently hating girls. In any event, the father (for males) is the symbol of the norms of society; he identifies symbolically right from wrong. If the process proceeds naturally, the little boy will develop normally, that is, develop a strong superego capable of controlling the id. However, if the father is cruel or if there is no father figure (note that a biological father is unnecessary), the little boy will not identify with the father and thus will not internalize the norms or authority of society. In other words, he will not develop a strong superego capable of controlling the id.

Needless to say, the process does not work in exactly the same way for little girls. Freud resolved the obvious difficulty by suggesting that females had "penis envy" and reacted to a fear of symbolic castration. Other than overreacting and identifying with the mother, who, for little girls, represents the norms of society, the rest of the process operates the same way.

Individuals who do not successfully resolve the Oedipal or Electra complex and thus do not develop a strong superego capable of controlling the id were called psychopaths by Freud. (Sociologists call them sociopaths.)[33] Many criminal offenders are presumed to be *psychopaths*, *sociopaths*, or *antisocial personalities*[34] and are characterized by no sense of guilt, no subjective conscience, and no sense of right and wrong. They have difficulty in forming relationships with other people; they cannot empathize with other people. Here is an extended list of characteristics of psychopaths:[35]

1. Superficial charm and good "intelligence"
2. Absence of delusions and other signs of irrational "thinking"
3. Absence of "nervousness" or psychoneurotic manifestations
4. Unreliability
5. Untruthfulness and insincerity
6. Lack of remorse or shame
7. Inadequately motivated antisocial behavior
8. Poor judgment and failure to learn by experience
9. Pathologic egocentricity and incapacity for love
10. General poverty in major affective reactions
11. Specific loss of insight
12. Unresponsiveness in general interpersonal relations
13. Fantastic and uninviting behavior, with drink and sometimes without
14. Suicide rarely carried out
15. Sex life impersonal, trivial, and poorly integrated
16. Failure to follow any life plan

Samuel Yochelson (1906–1976) and Stanton Samenow (1941–) have developed a theory of the criminal personality that, in many respects, is similar to the theory of the psychopath.[36] The criminal personality and the psychopath share many of the same characteristics. A notable difference between the two theories is that individuals with a criminal personality, according to Yochelson and Samenow, freely choose to commit their crimes, whereas the psychopath's behavior is presumed to be determined by psychological factors (most notably in Freud's view by an unresolved Oedipal or Electra complex). Another difference between the two theories is that fear (of embarrassment, injury, and death) is a key component of the criminal personality but not of the psychopath.

Finally, a fourth deep-seated problem of which crime has been considered symptomatic is an unconscious desire for punishment. In "Criminality from a Sense of Guilt" (1915), Freud described the phenomenon.[37] He suggested that some people, with a strong or overdeveloped superego, commit crimes in order to be caught and punished—not for the crime for which they had been caught, but for something that they had done in the past about which they felt guilty and for which they were not caught or punished. Obviously, this theory does not explain the large numbers of successful criminals.

The principal policy implication of considering crime symptomatic of deep-seated problems is to provide psychotherapy or psychoanalysis. *Psychoanalysis* is a procedure, first developed by Freud, that among other things attempts to make patients conscious or aware of unconscious and deep-seated problems to resolve the symptoms associated with them. Methods used include a variety of projective tests (such as the interpretation of Rorschach inkblots), dream interpretation, and free association. Another policy implication that derives logically from Freudian theory is to provide people with legal outlets to sublimate or redirect their sexual and aggressive drives.

In addition to the theories attributed to the work of Freud, other psychoanalytic theories of criminality can be inferred from the work of some his followers or the neo-Freudians. Many of the neo-Freudians differed with Freud over the primacy of sexual and aggressive drives in the motivation of human behavior and its disorders. Again, it is important to emphasize that the theorists identified here were not concerned with crime per se and that the theories of criminality attributed to them are inferred from what they had to say about personality disorders in general.

Alfred Adler (1870–1937) maintained that the source of personality disorder and, for purposes of this discussion, criminality was a fear of inferiority and a compensatory drive for power and superiority. Thus, for example, the rapist achieves power and superiority over his victim to compensate for his own fear of inferiority.

Erik Erikson (1902–1994) believed that the root of personality abnormality and, for purposes of this discussion, criminality is in an inadequate development of a sense of identity or the result of a sense of inferiority or inadequacy. Many offenders, especially gang members, commit their crimes to gain notoriety, or a "rep" (reputation). In this view, they do so to overcome their sense of inferiority or inadequacy.

Karen Horney (1885–1952) asserted that the root of personality disorder and, for purposes of this discussion, criminality is in a basic anxiety—the feeling of being isolated and helpless in a potentially hostile world—and a need for security. Many people find the problems in their lives overwhelming and are scared and anxious about them. Everyone desires security, and criminal behavior is one way of achieving it, if only temporarily.

Finally, Erich Fromm (1900–1980) argued that the root of personality abnormality and, for purposes of this discussion, criminality is in the need for belongingness, or being connected to other human beings. Isolation and aloneness are major threats. Children, especially, need security; they need to feel that they belong in a family. But as individuals mature, they are impelled by another motive: the desire for freedom, to escape from the very restrictions that provide the security. Thus, delinquent behavior may satisfy the need for belongingness. That may explain why so much delinquency is committed by groups of youths. Adult criminality may be committed out of a desire for freedom. Perhaps, at no other time in their lives are individuals as free as when they are committing crime. If they are alone in their pursuits, no one is telling them what to do; they do not have to answer to anybody but themselves.

Psychoanalysis and the psychoanalytic theory on which it is based are components of a medical model of crime causation that has, to varying degrees, informed criminal justice policy in the United States for a century. The general conception of this medical model is that criminals are biologically or, in this case, psychologically "sick" and in need of treatment.

GENERAL PROBLEMS
WITH PSYCHOANALYTIC THEORIES

First, although evidence indicates that at least some criminal offenders have psychological problems, the bulk of the research on the issue suggests that most criminals are not psychologically disturbed or, at least, no more disturbed than the rest of the population.[38] Few criminal offenders have major psychiatric disorders.[39]

For example, Bromberg and Thompson examined ten thousand felons in New York City and classified 1.5 percent as psychotic (*psychoses* are severe mental disorders characterized by personality disintegration and loss of contact with reality), 6.9 percent as psychoneurotic (*neuroses* are emotional disorders characterized by loss of joy in living and overuse of defense mechanisms against anxiety), 6.9 percent as psychopathic, 2.4 percent as feebleminded, and 82.3 percent as normal.[40] Schuessler and Cressey summarized the results of 113 studies in which personality test scores of delinquents and criminals were compared with the scores of control groups.[41] They reported that not a single trait was shown to be more characteristic of one group than the other.[42] Monahan and Steadman found that "when proper controls are introduced for age, sex, social class, and other life history factors, criminals as a group experience no more mental illness than do other groups in society."[43]

Still, some evidence, some of it relatively recent, suggests that crime and psychological disturbance may be related. For example, Waldo and Dinitz examined ninety-four studies conducted between 1950 and 1965.[44] Unlike the previous studies mentioned, they found that of the ninety-four studies that they examined, of which twenty-nine used the Minnesota Multiphasic Personality Inventory (MMPI), seventy-six (81 percent) reported a psychological difference between criminals and noncriminals. However, Waldo and Dinitz warned that the findings were far from conclusive. Rosner found that 75 percent of the forty-five adolescents accused of murder and manslaughter that he examined could be diagnosed as being mentally ill.[45] Both Link and his associates and Steury report that people diagnosed as mentally ill are found in official arrest and court statistics at a rate greater than what would be expected given their numbers in the population.[46] In both studies, however, the authors emphasize that the relationship is a "modest" one and that the vast majority of known criminals are not psychologically disturbed. The findings of Link et al. and Steury may be more a function of differential processing than of a significant relationship between psychological disturbance and criminality.

Even if the relationship is not the product of differential processing by criminal justice authorities, it nevertheless suggests a second problem. If a person who commits a crime has a psychological disturbance, that does not mean that the psychological disturbance causes the crime. Many people with psychological disturbances do not commit crimes, and many people without psychological disturbances do commit crimes.[47]

Third, there are problems with psychotherapy and the theory on which it is based. For example, psychoanalytic theory and psychotherapy as an approach to rehabilitation generally focus on the individual offender and not on the individual offender in interaction with the environment in which the criminal behavior occurs.[48] Criminal behavior is considered a personal problem and not a social one. Yet, the personality may not play a significant role in the cause of criminal behavior.[49] The theory also suggests that the personality is set in early childhood and remains relatively stable over time. This may not be true and seems to preclude the possibility of personality change.

Psychotherapy rests on faith. Much of its theoretical structure is scientifically untestable. Unconscious processes, which play such a major role in psychoanalytic theories, can only be measured indirectly.

Psychoanalytic theories of crime have also been criticized for being based on circular reasoning. That is, criminal behavior is presumed to be caused by mental illness which, itself, is indicated by the criminal behavior.[50]

Another criticism of Freud's theory has to do with its generalizability. The theory is based on Freud's work with mostly upper-middle-class and upper-class female patients.[51] Some critics wonder whether the theory applies equally well to other types of people.

The behaviors that are treated in psychotherapy are not criminal; they are the deep-seated problems.[52] Criminal behavior is assumed to be symptomatic of the deep-seated problems. That assumption may not be true. Many people who do not engage in crime have deep-seated problems, and many people who do not have deep-seated problems do engage in crime.

Another problem is that psychoanalytic "talking therapies" require the client to have a reasonable level of verbal intelligence,[53] an ability that many criminal offenders lack. A related problem is that psychotherapy rests on the assumption that if people change their verbal behavior (through psychotherapy), they will change their actual behavior.[54] That assumption may not be true. What people say and do often are very different.

Most psychotherapies also require the client to be strongly motivated to sit through weekly (or more frequent) sessions for a year or longer.[55] Many criminal offenders do not have the necessary motivation to complete (or to engage in) the lengthy process. From a practical standpoint, even if criminal offenders were motivated to complete the lengthy process, the delivery of long-term psychotherapy, especially the one-on-one variety, is too expensive and inefficient to be used widely in correctional settings anyway.[56] Perhaps the most telling problem is that people who receive psychiatric and psychoanalytical treatment generally are no more likely to be cured than people who do not receive such treatment.[57]

Many years ago, in reviewing the impact of psychiatry on corrections, Tappan made an observation that is still relevant today:

> The focus upon mental pathology has resulted in a conception of criminals as sick people. . . . The prevalent idea of criminal illness is highly misleading. Criminals are not generally neurotic, psychotic, or psychopathic. . . . Worse, by merely attaching a general label to the offender, one may be led to assume quite erroneously that the problem has been solved thereby or that it is necessary only to provide some vague psychotherapy to resolve the difficulty.[58]

HUMANISTIC
PSYCHOLOGICAL THEORY

Humanistic psychological theory refers primarily to the work of Abraham Maslow and Seymour Halleck. The theories of Maslow and Halleck are fundamentally psychoanalytic, but here they are called humanistic because they assume that human beings are basically good even though sometimes they are constrained by society to act badly. By contrast, the Freudian theories assume that human beings are inherently bad, motivated by sexual and aggressive drives.

Abraham Maslow (1908–1970) attempted to integrate into a single theoretical framework insights from some of the neo-Freudians discussed previously. From his own experiences as a therapist, he believed that each of the neo-Freudians, from whom he adopted material, was correct for various people at various times. Like the theorists described in the previous section, Maslow did not apply his theory to crime per se, and so, as was done in the last section, inferences are made from Maslow's work about what he would have said about the causes of crime had he addressed the subject.

Maslow postulated that human beings are motivated by a *need hierarchy* comprising five basic levels of needs.[59] The most basic of the needs are the physiological ones (food, water, and procreational sex). Next are the safety needs (security, stability, freedom from fear, anxiety, chaos, and so forth) followed, in order, by the belongingness and love needs, the esteem needs (self-esteem and the esteem of others), and, finally, the need for self-actualization (being what one can, being true to one's nature, becoming everything that one is capable of becoming). According to Maslow, during a given period a person's life is dominated by a particular need. It remains dominated by that need until the need has been relatively satisfied, at which time a new need emerges to dominate the person's life. From this view, crime may be understood as a means by which individuals satisfy their basic human needs. They choose crime because they cannot satisfy their needs legally or, for whatever reason, choose not to satisfy their needs legally.

An obvious crime prevention implication of the theory is to help people satisfy their basic human needs in legitimate ways. In his presidential address to the Academy of Criminal Justice Sciences, Francis Cullen (1951–) argued that the relatively high crime rates in the United States, compared to other industrialized nations, are at least partly the result of inadequate social support.[60] Social support is the provision, both the perceived and the actual provision, of such diverse things as material aid, financial assistance, advice, guidance, emotional support, feedback, social reinforcement, and socializing.[61] Cullen notes that social support can occur at different social levels: "Micro-level support can be delivered by a confiding individual, such as a spouse or a best friend. But social support also can be viewed as a property of social networks and of communities and larger ecological units in which individuals are enmeshed."[62]

Cullen, sounding very much like a radical criminologist (he maintains that "notions of social support appear in diverse criminological writings"), concludes his address by criticizing "the excessive individualism in the United States, which too often degenerates into a politics justifying either the crass pursuit of rights or materialistic self-aggrandizement."[63] He notes that "in this context, there is a lack of attention to the public good, service to others, and an appreciation for our need for connectedness."[64] Thus, his address is "a call to revitalize our common bonds and to build a society supportive of all its citizens."[65] Maslow likely would agree.

Seymour L. Halleck (1929–) views crime as one among several different adaptations to the helplessness caused by oppression.[66] For Halleck, there are two general types of oppression, objective and subjective. Each has two subtypes. The subtypes of objective oppression are social oppression (for example, oppression resulting from racial discrimination) and the oppression that occurs in two-person interactions (for instance, a parent's unfair restriction of a child's activities). The subtypes of subjective oppression are oppression from within (guilt from the superego) and projected or misunderstood oppression (a person's feeling of being oppressed when, in fact, he or she is not).

For Halleck, the subjective emotional experience of either type of oppression is helplessness, which is adapted to by the individual in one of six different ways. Some people adapt to the feeling of helplessness by simply conforming, that is, accepting the oppression and feeling of helplessness; sometimes suffering in silence; accepting the rules of society. Other people adapt through activism, that is, active efforts to change the environment by following the rules. Halleck notes that a combination of conformity and activism generally is considered normal by society. Another adaptation is a different type of activism where the individual attempts to change the environment by legal attempts to change the rules of society. Mental illness, which involves an indirect effort to change the environment through the communication of suffering, is a fifth possible adaptation, and criminality is the sixth type. Criminality is the attempt to change the environment by illegally breaking the rules of society or by creating new but illegal rules.

Halleck suggests that the criminal adaptation is more likely when alternative adaptations are not possible or are blocked by other people.

He also maintains that criminal behavior sometimes is chosen as an adaptation over other possible alternatives because it offers gratifications (psychological advantages) that could not be achieved otherwise.[67] Halleck lists fourteen psychological advantages of crime:[68]

1. The adaptational advantages of crime in changing one's environment are more desirable than illness or conformity.

2. Crime involves activity, and when man is engaged in motoric behavior, he feels less helpless.

3. However petty a criminal act may be, it carries with it a promise of change in a favorable direction.

4. During the planning and execution of a criminal act the offender is a free man. (He is immune from the oppressive dictates of others.)

5. Crime offers the possibility of excitement.

6. Crime calls for the individual to maximize his faculties and talents which might otherwise lie dormant.

7. Crime can relieve feelings of inner oppression and stress.

8. Crime increases external stresses which allows the individual to concentrate upon these threats to his equilibrium and temporarily allows him to abandon his chronic intrapsychic problems.

9. Once a person has convinced himself that the major pressures in his life come from without, there is less tendency to blame himself for his failures.

10. Adopting the criminal role provides an excellent rationalization for inadequacy.

11. Crime has a more esteemed social status than mental illness.

12. America has an ambivalent attitude toward crime. Although crime is regularly condemned, it is also glamorized.

13. Deviant behavior sometimes helps the criminal to form close and relatively nonoppressive relations with other criminals.

14. Crime can provide pleasure or gratify needs.

Halleck's theory suggests at least three crime prevention implications. First, sources of social oppression should be eliminated wherever possible. Second, alternative, legal ways of coping with oppression must be provided. Third, psychotherapy should be provided for subjective oppressions.

Besides some of the general criticisms of positivist theories and psychotherapy listed in the last section, a major problem with the theories of both Maslow and Halleck is that they do not go far enough. That is, they do not identify and analyze the sources of need deprivation (in Maslow's theory) and objective oppression (in Halleck's theory) and their more fundamental relationship to criminality, however defined.

STUDY QUESTIONS

1. What is the relationship between intelligence and criminality *and* delinquency?
2. In Freudian theory, what is crime? What are examples of causes of crime in Freudian theory?
3. What are causes of crime according to neo–Freudian theories?
4. How would Maslow explain crime?
5. How would Halleck explain crime?
6. What are some crime prevention implications of psychological/ psychoanalytic theories?
7. What are some general problems with psychological/ psychoanalytic theories of crime causation?
8. How do psychological/psychoanalytic theories of crime causation compare with theories previously described in this book?

NOTES

1. See Vold and Bernard (1986:72).
2. Vold and Bernard (1986:72).
3. See Vold and Bernard (1986:72); also see Gould (1981).
4. Vold (1979:83).
5. Quoted in Vold (1979:83).
6. Sutherland and Cressey (1974:152).
7. R. Gordon (1976); Hirschi and Hindelang (1977).
8. R. Gordon (1976); Hirschi and Hindelang (1977); also see Vold and Bernard (1986:77); Andrews and Bonta (1994:133). Note that the

studies dealt with delinquency and not adult criminality.
9. Hirschi and Hindelang (1977); also see Vold and Bernard (1986:78).
10. Also see Wilson and Herrnstein (1985:171 and Chap. 10); Denno (1985).
11. Levin (1997:291).
12. Also see Ellis and Walsh (1997). For a critique of *The Bell Curve* and by implication the other books, see Cullen et al. (1997).
13. The following description is from Rushton (1995) and Levin (1997).

14. The latter proposition is shared by social control theory, described in Chapter 6.

15. See Levin (1997:324–327).

16. See, for example, Morris (1998:326–328 and 22–23).

17. Salopek (1997).

18. Vold (1979:97); however, see Andrews and Bonta (1994:133) for a different view.

19. Vold (1979:97).

20. See Vold (1979:97); Cullen et al. (1997:402).

21. See Vold (1979:97); Cullen et al. (1997:391).

22. Unless indicated otherwise, material in this section is from Freud (1953); Hutchins (1952); Andrews and Bonta (1994); Woodworth and Sheehan (1964); Hall (1954). Theorists who have applied psychoanalytic theory to the explanation of crime and delinquency are Aichorn (1935); Healy and Bronner (1926, 1936); Alexander and Healy (1935); Abrahamsen (1944, 1960); Friedlander (1947); Redl and Wineman (1951, 1952).

23. Einstadter and Henry (1995:110).

24. Martin et al. (1990:79).

25. Note that this theory typically is considered a social control or learning theory. However, because of its use of Freud's defense mechanisms, it is introduced here.

26. Sykes and Matza (1957:666).

27. For a critique of this position, see Taylor et al. (1974:183–185).

28. Lanier and Henry (1998:150).

29. Lanier and Henry (1998:151); Beirne and Messerschmidt (2000:162).

30. Lanier and Henry (1998:151).

31. Andrews and Bonta (1994:74).

32. Andrews and Bonta (1994:74).

33. Although the two terms are frequently used interchangeably, some social scientists distinguish between them by arguing that *psychopaths* are the products of psychological or biological factors, such as an unresolved Oedipal or Electra complex, while *sociopaths* are the products of social factors, such as broken homes.

34. See Vold and Bernard (1986:122).

35. From Cleckley (1982). For a discussion of the evolution of the concept psychopathy in criminology, see Rafter (1997).

36. See Yochelson and Samenow (1976).

37. Also see Martin et al. (1990:78–79).

38. See Curran and Renzetti (1994:128).

39. Andrews and Bonta (1994:210).

40. Bromberg and Thompson (1937).

41. Schuessler and Cressey (1950).

42. Schuessler and Cressey (1950); but see Andrews and Bonta (1994:60) for a different interpretation.

43. Monahan and Steadman (1983); also see Vold and Bernard (1986:121).

44. Waldo and Dinitz (1967).

45. Rosner (1979).

46. Link et al. (1992); Steury (1993).

47. Curran and Renzetti (1994:110).

48. See Jeffery (1977:132, 138).

49. Vold and Bernard (1986:128); but see Andrews and Bonta (1994:63) for the opposite view.

50. Einstadter and Henry (1995:116–117); Curran and Renzetti (1994:128); Vold and Bernard (1986:116).

51. Martin et al. (1990:84).

52. See Jeffery (1977:138–139).

53. Andrews and Bonta (1994:195).

54. See Jeffery (1977:138).

55. Andrews and Bonta (1994:195).

56. Andrews and Bonta (1994:195).

57. Vold and Bernard (1986:117).

58. Tappan (1951:11).

59. Maslow (1970, originally published in 1954).

60. Cullen (1994).

61. Cullen (1994:530).

62. Cullen (1994:530–531); also see Chamlin and Cochran (1997) and DeFronzo (1997).

63. Cullen (1994:551).

64. Cullen (1994:551–552).

65. Cullen (1994:552). Cullen and Wright (1997) have recently combined social support theory and general strain theory (see Chap. 6).

66. Halleck (1967).

67. See Katz (1988) for a similar view.

68. Halleck (1967:76–80).

6

☒

Sociological Theories

THE CONTRIBUTIONS OF DURKHEIM

Many of the sociological theories of crime, actually delinquency causation (*sociological positivism*), have their roots in the work of the French sociologist Emile Durkheim (1858–1917).[1] Like Saint-Simon and Comte before him, Durkheim's theory emerged during a period of profound social change in France. French society was still recovering from the Revolution of 1789, Napoleon's defeat at Waterloo, and defeats in the Franco-Prussian War.[2] In addition, the Industrial Revolution was beginning to pick up steam.[3]

Durkheim rejected the idea that the world is simply the product of individual actions. His basic premise was that society is more than a simple aggregate of individuals; it is a reality *sui generis* (unique).[4] Rejecting the idea that social phenomena, like crime, can be explained solely by the biology or psychology of individuals, Durkheim argued instead that society is not the direct reflection of the characteristics of its individual members, because individuals cannot always choose.[5] For Durkheim, social laws and institutions are "social facts" that dominate individuals, and all people can do is submit to them. The coercion may be formal as, for example, by means of law, or informal as, for example, by means of peer pressure.[6] Like Comte before him, Durkheim maintained that, with the aid of positive science, all people can expect is to discover the direction or course of social laws so that they can adapt to them with the least amount of pain.

For Durkheim, crime, too, is a social fact.[7] It is a normal aspect of society, because it is found in all societies. Nevertheless, different types of societies should have greater or lesser degrees of it. Not only did Durkheim believe that crime is a normal aspect of society, he also believed that crime is functional for society.[8] He noted that crime marks the boundaries of morality.[9] In other words, people would not know what acceptable behavior was if it were not for crime. Crime also functions to promote social solidarity by uniting people against crime. In a sense, the punishment of criminals is the payoff to citizens who obey the law.[10] According to Durkheim, the social solidarity function of crime is so important that crime would have to be created if it did not already exist. Additionally, crime is functional because it provides a means of achieving necessary social change through, for example, civil disobedience and, under certain circumstances, directly contributes to social change, as, for example, in the repeal of prohibition.[11]

Much of Durkheim's attention was directed toward the changes occurring in society as it was becoming increasingly more complex and industrialized. An especially important aspect of those changes for him was the occupational specialization (that is, *division of labor*) that was becoming more commonplace. Durkheim argued that human beings are not free to choose, but rather live in a world characterized by a "forced division of labor" in which peoples' natural abilities generally are not used.[12] A product of such circumstances is anomie.

For Durkheim, *anomie* is the breakdown of social norms or the dissociation of the individual from the *collective conscience* or the general sense of morality of the times.[13] Anomie is the cause of crime and is expressed in two interrelated ways: *lack of regulation* and *lack of integration*.[14] In the former, the collective conscience is unable to regulate human desires; in the latter, "individualism" is promoted to such a degree that people become so selfish or egoistic that they no longer care about the welfare of other human beings. To reduce crime, Durkheim advocated the development of a spontaneous division of labor in which unmerited social inequities would not exist.[15] To help achieve this goal, Durkheim promoted the formation of occupational associations and the abolition of inheritance.[16]

As noted, many of the major sociological theories of delinquency[17] come directly from Durkheim's ideas. Among them are anomie or strain theory, differential opportunity theory, theories of culture conflict, cultural transmission and cultural deviance, social disorganization theory, functionalist theory, control theories, and social reaction theories.

THE THEORY
OF THE CHICAGO SCHOOL

In the 1920s, members of the Department of Sociology at the University of Chicago engaged in an effort to identify environmental factors associated with crime. Specifically, they attempted to uncover the relationship between a neighborhood's crime rate and the characteristics of the neighborhood. It was the first large-scale study of crime in the United States and was to serve as the basis for many future investigations into the causes of crime and delinquency.

The research of the Chicago School was based on a model taken from ecology; as a result, that school is sometimes called the Chicago School of Human Ecology.[18] *Ecology* is a branch of biology in which the interrelationship of plants and animals is studied in its natural environment.[19] In biology, this interrelationship is referred to as *symbiosis*. Robert Park (1864–1944) was the first of the Chicago theorists to propose this *organic* or *biological analogy,* that is, the similarity between the organization of plant and animal life in nature and the organization of human beings in societies.[20]

At the time, Chicago was the second largest city in the United States, with a population of over two million people. Its population had doubled every ten years between 1860 and 1910 as the result of industrialization and massive immigration.[21] Park and his colleague, Ernest Burgess (1886–1966), described the growth of American cities like Chicago in ecological terms. Although recognizing that natural and historical factors could influence their growth, Park and Burgess nonetheless argued that cities tend to grow radially from their center in concentric circles through a process of invasion, dominance, and succession.[22] That is, a cultural or ethnic group invades a territory occupied by another group and dominates that new territory until it is displaced or succeeded by another group, and the cycle repeats itself. As for the concentric circles, from the core to the periphery, zone 1 is the central business district or, in Chicago, the "Loop"; zone 2 is the transitional area, usually the slums; zone 3 is the area where the homes of blue-collar workers are located; zone 4 is a residential area of nicer single-family houses and expensive apartments; and zone 5 is the suburbs.[23]

This model of human ecology was used by other Chicago theorists, most notably Clifford R. Shaw (1896–1957) and Henry D. McKay (1899–1980) in their studies of juvenile delinquency in Chicago.[24] Shaw assumed that delinquents were basically normal human beings and that their delinquent behavior was caused by environmental factors peculiar to specific neighborhoods. To test his theory, Shaw examined police and court records to find neighborhoods with the most delinquents. He then analyzed the characteristics of those neighborhoods. To aid them in their investigation, Shaw, together with McKay, created three types of maps: (1) "spot maps" that located the residences of the youth in police and court records, (2) "rate maps" that showed the percentage of the total juvenile population in 140-square-mile areas that had police or court records, and (3) "zone maps" that showed the rates of male juvenile delinquency within the concentric zones of the city.

An analysis of the maps showed that zone 2 consistently had the highest rates of delinquency in the city despite almost complete turnovers in the ethnic composition of the population living in that zone. Thus, for example, in 1884, approximately 90 percent of the population in zone 2 was Irish, German, Scandinavian, Scottish, or English, and the children of those groups had the highest rates of delinquency in Chicago. By 1930, 85 percent of zone 2 was Italian, Polish, Slavic, or Czech—almost a complete turnover, and the children of those groups had the highest rates of delinquency in Chicago. Furthermore, when the ethnic groups moved out of zone 2, the high delinquency rates did not follow them. In short, something about zone 2 produced high delinquency rates regardless of the ethnic composition of the population that lived there.

Shaw also discovered that even in the worst neighborhoods in zone 2, only about 20 percent of the youths had police or court records. Therefore, he began to assemble extensive "life histories" of individual delinquents to discover what environmental factors affected their behavior. From the life histories,[25] he confirmed that most of the delinquents were not much different from nondelinquents with regard to personality traits, physical condition, and intelligence. He did find that the areas of high delinquency were "socially disorganized." For the

Chicago theorists, *social disorganization* is the condition in which (1) the usual controls over delinquents are largely absent, (2) delinquent behavior often is approved of by parents and neighbors, (3) many opportunities are available for delinquent behavior, and (4) little encouragement, training, or opportunity exists for legitimate employment.[26]

Shaw also discovered that delinquent activities began as play activities at an early age, that older boys taught these activities to younger boys, that the normal methods of official social control could not stop this process, and that it was only later in a delinquent career that a boy identified himself with the criminal world.[27] In sum, Shaw and his colleagues concluded that delinquency was the product of a "detachment from conventional groups"—a term nearly synonymous with Durkheim's concept of lack of integration—caused by social disorganization in certain areas of the city. As noted earlier, the theory is sometimes referred to as social disorganization theory.

Because Shaw believed that juvenile delinquency was caused by social disorganization, he did not think that individual treatment of delinquents would be effective in reducing the problem.[28] So, in 1932, Shaw and his colleagues established the Chicago Area Project (CAP), which was designed to prevent delinquency through the organization and empowerment of neighborhood residents.[29] Twenty-two neighborhood centers, staffed and controlled by local residents, were established in six areas of Chicago. The centers had two principal functions. One was to coordinate community resources such as schools, churches, labor unions, and industries to solve community problems, and the other was to sponsor activity programs such as scouts, summer camps, and sports leagues to develop a positive interest by individuals in their own welfare and to unite citizens to solve their own problems. For a quarter of a century, the Chicago Area Project served neighborhoods of Chicago and only ceased operation in 1957 following Shaw's death.[30] Evaluations of the project suggest that it had a negligible effect on delinquency.[31]

One of the problems with the theory of the Chicago School is the presumed relationship among social disorganization, detachment from conventional groups, and delinquency. The relationship may be a spurious one. In other words, other factors may contribute to social disorganization, detachment from conventional groups, and delinquency that make them appear to be related to each other when, in fact, they are not (remember the relationship between the sale of ice cream and the homicide rate?).

In this regard, one must ask, Why do cities develop in the way that they do? Why do delinquency areas emerge in certain areas of the city? Are delinquency areas inherent in the growth of cities? Most cities do not grow randomly. Their growth is predicated on the values and decisions of political and economic elites. The early Chicago neighborhoods, for example, were planned with great deliberation. One of the factors that contributes to the decline of city neighborhoods is the decades-old practice of *redlining* where banks refuse to lend money for home improvements in an area because of the race or ethnicity of the inhabitants.[32] What usually occurs in redlined areas (a practice, incidentally, that still occurs today despite its illegality) is that neighborhood and property values decline dramatically until they reach a point where land speculators and developers, usually in conjunction with political leaders, buy the land for urban renewal or gentrification and make fortunes in the process. In short, political and economic elites may cause social disorganization, detachment from conventional groups, and delinquency, perhaps not intentionally, by the conscious decisions that they make.[33]

The Chicago theorists did not challenge the destructive practices of Chicago's political and economic elite; thus, they merely addressed the symptoms of the problem rather than its causes.[34] In so doing, the Chicago theorists revealed their own timidity (perhaps they were coopted or "bought off"), antiurban bias, and romanticism—yearning for a return to village life and the social controls of communal living.[35]

From an entirely different vantage point, the Chicago theorists can be criticized for suggesting that certain inner-city neighborhoods were socially disorganized in the first place. Sutherland, who is discussed later in the section on learning theories, recognized this problem when he substituted in his own theory the concept of "differential social organization" for the Chicago School's social disorganization. To call a particular area socially disorganized is to impose one's own values of what constitutes social organization (usually the values of the dominant culture) and to fail to appreciate that an area may be organized differentially based on a different set of values, especially the values of the people who live in the area.[36] In short, critics suggest that the Chicago theorists observed diversity in social organization but, in light of their own biases, interpreted what they saw as social disorganization.[37]

Another related problem was the organic or biological analogy used by the Chicago theorists to describe the development of society.[38] Human society, as noted, is regulated by cultural and legal forces that only superficially resemble the forces that govern the survival of the fittest in nature. In their apparent naivete, the Chicago theorists neglected to consider the effects of political struggle on social change.[39]

Overprediction is another problem. The Chicago theorists never could adequately explain why only a relatively small percentage of youths in the delinquency areas actually became delinquent. Even within areas that were considered socially disorganized, there were groups, such as Asians or European Jews, whose children did not have high rates of delinquency.[40] If social disorganization and detachment from conventional groups were such powerful causes of delinquency, then why were not more youths affected by their influence? Social disorganization theory also does not explain especially bizarre delinquent behaviors (such as those thought to be evidence of mental illness) very well.[41]

The overprediction problem might be related to another one: the use of official police and court records to measure delinquency in a given area.[42] Perhaps the official records did not capture the true extent of delinquency in an area because many of the youths who engaged in delinquent activities escaped detection or official processing. On the other hand, neighborhoods in zone 2 may have evidenced the most delinquency because the official statistics do not capture much delinquency in middle- and upper-class neighborhoods.

The theory of the Chicago School has also been criticized for being based on circular reasoning.[43] That is, social disorganization is the cause of delinquency, and delinquency is an indicator of social disorganization.

Finally, there is the ecological fallacy and the problem with the utility of the theory. The *ecological fallacy* refers to the explanation of one level of analysis based on the examination of a different level of analysis (for instance, the explanation of individual behavior based on a study of group rates).[44] The Chicago theorists based their analysis on group rates and so, for example, they found that neighborhoods in zone 2 had the highest rates of delinquency. The problem is that the theory does not allow the prediction, with any degree of certainty, of who among those youths living in zone 2 is likely to become delinquent.[45] The theory's usefulness, therefore, is diminished.

Before leaving the theory of the Chicago School, consider two derivatives of the theory. The first is exemplified by the work of architect Oscar Newman (1935–), *Defensible Space: Crime Prevention Through Urban Design*.[46] In his book, Newman extends the theory of the Chicago School to a consideration of the actual physical form of the urban environment and how that form affects crime. For example, he reports that poorly designed buildings and surroundings of low- and middle-income housing projects have crime rates much higher than better designed projects that have similar types of residents and densities.

Defensible space is a model for residential environments designed to inhibit criminality through a range of mechanisms that include "real and symbolic barriers, strongly defined areas of influence, and improved opportunities for surveillance." The goal, like that of the Chicago Area

Project before it, is to reduce crime by bringing the environment under the control of its residents. The idea of increasing surveillance, incidentally, is the basis for the popular neighborhood watch programs.[47]

In January 1995, Henry G. Cisneros, then Secretary of Housing and Urban Development (HUD), published a widely distributed essay lauding the merits of defensible space. Cisneros recognizes that defensible space is not a "cure-all" for the problems of crime and delinquency in inner-city neighborhoods and admits that structural changes are necessary to affect the crime problem as a whole. Nevertheless, he believes that "the practical successes of defensible space initiatives [and] the fact that they can be implemented quickly and require very little public funding . . . make defensible space an approach well worth our consideration."[48]

According to both Cisneros and Newman, the most promising applications of the defensible space concept are to neighborhoods that are deteriorating but continue to "retain residents and other stakeholders who still have hope that traumatic decline can be prevented."[49] They are less optimistic about devastated areas of older cities where a sense of community has all but disappeared.

Despite Cisneros's optimism about the utility of defensible space, Wilson and Herrnstein warn that although "there are physical changes that may reduce the rates of some kinds of crime . . . [t]he role played in this reduction by such factors . . . remains unclear."[50]

Another derivative of the theory of the Chicago School is the routine activity theory of Lawrence E. Cohen (1945–) and Marcus Felson (1947–). Cohen and Felson's "routine activity approach" to criminality extends human ecology analysis to the explanation of crime and victimization rates over time.[51] For Cohen and Felson, structural changes in the routine activities of everyday life affect crimes against both persons and property. Structural changes in routine activities influence those crimes through their effect on any one of three factors: (1) "motivated offenders" (for example, teenage boys, unemployed people, drug addicts), (2) "suitable targets" (such as unlocked homes or cars), and (3) "the absence of capable guardians against a violation" (for instance, the absence of police officers, homeowners, security systems).[52] Cohen and Felson maintain that all three of the factors are necessary for the successful completion of crimes.[53] It is important to emphasize that Cohen and Felson do not attempt to explain criminal motivation but, instead, assume that all people will commit crime unless they are prevented from doing so. Criminal activities are viewed, by Cohen and Felson, as routine activities. They conclude that crime is so rooted in the legitimate opportunity structure of our society and in the freedom and prosperity that many people enjoy, that to reduce crime will require substantial modifications in our everyday way of life.[54]

Thus, the crime prevention implications of routine activity theory focus on potential crime victims who must change their lifestyles so they are no longer such easy targets for criminal offenders. Much of the emphasis is on securing the immediate environment through the creation of defensible space, target hardening, and increasing the presence of capable guardians. Also implied in the theory, though deemphasized by its authors, is increasing legitimate opportunities—a principal crime prevention implication of anomie theories (which are discussed later in this chapter).

Routine activity theory has been criticized for its assumption that all people will commit crime unless they are prevented from doing so—an assumption that this theory shares with social control theories (which are discussed later in this chapter). Some criminologists take issue with the theory's assumption that criminal motivation is rooted in human nature.[55]

Another problem with routine activity theory is that it fails to explain its key concept—routine activities. In other words, the theory does not specify which routine activities, or which type of such activities, affect crimes.[56] Do all routine activities affect crimes? Do all routine activities influence the number of motivated offenders, the availability of suitable targets, or the degree of guardianship? Probably not. In addition, the theory does not specify how the three key concepts interact to affect crime. It treats them as equally important, which they probably are not. The theory, as formulated, has also been criticized for being applicable only to "ordinary" predatory crime.[57]

A problem with the crime prevention implications of routine activity theory or, specifically, with its focus on securing the immediate environment, is that such a strategy is likely only to displace the criminal activity of motivated offenders to less secure environments.[58] This is a problem with Newman's defensible space concept as well. Thus, taken to its logical conclusion, the theory creates a siege mentality in which people who can afford it secure themselves against crime, leaving those people who cannot afford it to fare for themselves as best they can. It also creates the justification for an Orwellian society in which surveillance of the population is pervasive and privacy is a rare commodity. Finally, routine activity theory has been criticized for coming close to blaming the victim. In suggesting that a solution to the crime problem depends on potential victims changing their routine activities, the theory implies that the routine activities of women, for example, are what causes rape and sexual assault—an implication that many people, particularly feminist critics, find offensive.[59]

FUNCTIONALISM

Talcott Parsons (1902–1979), a Harvard sociologist, is credited with the introduction of functional theory, or structural-functional theory, in the United States in 1937.[60] At the time, the United States and other western industrial societies were in the midst of the worst depression ever experienced and on the verge of World War II.[61] Many observers believed that free enterprise had failed and that capitalism was doomed to either socialism on the left or fascism on the right.[62] Within this context, Parsons and his colleagues at Harvard engaged in an effort to produce a theory of society that would aid in the preservation of the free enterprise system (capitalism) and, of course, their privileged way of life. The result was functionalist theory, and its basic premise is as follows: the world is a system of interrelated parts, and each part makes a necessary contribution to the viability of the system (a *systems model* of society).[63] Crime, in this view, is a necessary part of the system (an idea borrowed from Durkheim).

To illustrate this theory as it is applies to crime, consider the explanation of the latent functions of female prostitution by Kingsley Davis (1908–1997), a student of Parsons and a former president of the American Sociological Association. Functions are presumed to be either manifest (intended) or latent (unintended and often unrecognized).[64] In describing its latent functions, Davis identifies the ways that prostitution contributes to the viability of the social system—a not so obvious relationship that can only be revealed by the well-trained and astute social scientist.[65]

Davis points out that prostitution functions to satisfy sexual desires with little psychic or financial investment.[66] It requires neither emotional involvement nor the expense associated with dating and marriage. More importantly, prostitution helps preserve the institution of the family and the aura of the "good" girl by relieving wives and girlfriends of the chore of satisfying their husbands' and boyfriends' "perverse" sexual desires. It also allows a small number of women to service a multitude of lusting single men in society, including the less desirable among them. Finally, prostitution is functional even for prostitutes themselves because in few other occupations can they earn as much. Similar functionalist arguments have been made for the urban political machine and even for poverty.[67]

Nearly one hundred years before Parsons, Karl Marx anticipated the functionalist argument. In a passage dripping with irony, Marx wrote:

> The criminal produces not only crimes, but also criminal law, and with this also the professor who gives lectures on criminal law, and

in addition to this the inevitable compendium in which this same professor throws his lectures onto the general market as "commodities.". . . The criminal moreover produces the whole of the police and of criminal justice, constables, judges, hangmen, juries, etc.; and all these different lines of business, which form equally many categories of the social division of labor, develop different capacities of the human spirit, create new needs and new ways of satisfying them. Torture alone has given rise to the most ingenious mechanical inventions, and employed many honorable craftsmen in the production of its instruments. . . . Crime takes a part of the superfluous population off the labor market and thus reduces competition among the laborers—up to a certain point preventing wages from falling below the minimum—the struggle against crime absorbs another part of this population. Thus the criminal comes in as one of those natural "counterweights" which bring about a correct balance and open up a whole perspective of "useful" occupations.

The effects of the criminal on the development of productive power can be shown in detail. Would locks ever have reached their present degree of excellence had there been no thieves? Would the making of banknotes have reached its present perfection had there been no forgers? . . . Crime, through its constantly new methods of attack on property, constantly calls into being new methods of defense, and so is as productive as strikes for the invention of machines. And if one leaves the sphere of private crime: would the world market ever have come into being but for national crime?[68]

Because functionalist theorists view crime as an integral part of society, necessary for its existence, they do not want to prevent crime. They only want to contain it within acceptable boundaries so that it does not destroy society.[69]

One of the more obvious problems with functionalist theory is that it fails to ask the question, Functional for whom? Who is the system? Failure to entertain this question inhibits the exploration of just how a particular phenomenon, such as crime, affects different groups within society.[70] This problem stems from a second one: the erroneous assumption that there is a consensus in society over moral values. The theory ignores social conflict.[71] A third problem is the inherent class bias of the theory. It promotes the "system" and social stability, regardless of how oppressive the system might be, over alternative social arrangements and social change.[72] A fourth and related problem is that the conception of social order in functionalist theory is based on elite definitions and not the definitions of the average citizen.[73] Thus, a fifth problem is that the "system" is viewed as greater or more important than the individuals that constitute it.[74] Functionalist theory, in short, is an elitist and politically conservative ideology.[75]

Other problems with functionalist theory are that it presents a view of society that often bears little resemblance to the society most people experience, its empirical work is based largely on secondary sources, it ignores the criminalization process (that is, how the established power structure creates crime), and it is untestable.[76] Regarding testability, how could one possibly falsify a functionalist proposition?

ANOMIE OR STRAIN THEORY

Like functionalists, anomie or strain theorists use a systems model to describe society. However, unlike functionalists, anomie theorists do not believe that all phenomena in society are functional. They believe that some phenomena are dysfunctional, that there are contradictions in society.[77]

In an article published in 1938, one year after Parsons introduced functionalist theory in the United States, Robert K. Merton (1910–), who was mentored by Talcott Parsons at Harvard,[78] observed that a major contradiction existed in the United States between cultural goals and the social structure. Adopting but also reformulating Durkheim's concept, he called the contradiction *anomie*. Specifically, Merton argued that in the United States the cultural goal of achieving wealth is deemed possible for all citizens even though the social structure limits the legitimate institutionalized means available for obtaining the goal.[79] For Merton, legitimate institutionalized means are the Protestant work ethic (that is, hard work, education, and deferred gratification); illegitimate means are force and fraud.[80] Because the social structure effectively limits the availability of legitimate institutionalized means, a *strain* is placed on people (hence the other name of the theory). Merton believed that strain could affect people in all social classes, but he acknowledged that it would most likely affect members of the lower class.[81]

Merton believed that individuals adapt to the problem of anomie or strain in one of several different ways: (1) conformity, (2) innovation, (3) ritualism, (4) retreatism, or (5) rebellion.[82] According to Merton, most people adapt by conforming; they "play the game."[83] Conformers pursue the cultural goal of wealth only through legitimate institutional means. Innovation is the adaptation at the root of most crime. After rejecting legitimate institutional means, innovators pursue the cultural goal of wealth through illegitimate means. Ritualism is the adaptation of the individual who "takes no chances," usually a member of the lower middle class. Ritualists do not actively pursue the cultural goal of wealth (they are willing to settle for less, oftentimes hoping that their children will succeed where they have not) but follow the legitimate institutional means anyway. Retreatists include alcoholics, drug addicts, psychotics, and other outcasts of society. Retreatists "drop out"; they do not pursue the cultural goal of wealth, so they do not employ legitimate institutional means. When their behavior is defined as criminal, retreatists are also a source of crime. Last is the adaptation of rebellion. Rebels reject both the cultural goal of wealth and the legitimate institutional means of achieving it and substitute both different goals and different means. Rebellion can be another source of crime.

In summary, Merton believed that a source of some, but not all, crime and delinquency was anomie or strain,[84] a disjunction or contradiction between the cultural goal of achieving wealth and the social structure's ability to provide legitimate institutional means of achieving the goal.

Beginning in the mid-1950s, renewed concern developed over the problem of juvenile gangs. Albert K. Cohen (1918–), a student of both Merton and Sutherland, adapted Merton's anomie or strain theory to his attempt to explain gang delinquency.[85] Cohen argued that delinquent acts generally were engaged in by gangs rather than individually and that, unlike adult criminality which is usually utilitarian (serves a useful purpose), gang delinquency was mostly nonutilitarian, malicious, and negativistic.[86] Two other important characteristics of the delinquent gang's subculture were "short-run hedonism" ("there is little interest in long-run goals") and "group autonomy" ("intolerance of restraint except from the informal pressures within the group itself").[87] In attempting to explain gang delinquency, Cohen surmised that it was to gain status among peers or the result of status frustration.[88] Thus, Cohen substituted the goal of status among peers for Merton's goal of achieving wealth.[89]

For Cohen, anomie or strain is experienced by juveniles who are unable to achieve status among peers by socially acceptable means (or "middle-class measuring rods"), such as family name and position in the community or academic or athletic achievement.[90] In response to the strain, either they can conform to middle-class values, generated primarily through the public school, and resign themselves to their subordinate position among their peers, or they can rebel (psychologists call it "reaction-formation") and establish their own value structures by turning middle-class values on their head.[91] These new value structures frequently promote the nonutilitarian, malicious, and negativistic behavior described by Cohen. Juveniles who rebel in this way tend to find each other and to form groups or gangs to validate and reinforce their new values.[92] Like Merton, Cohen believed that anomie can affect juveniles of any social class but that it disproportionately affects juveniles from the lower class.[93]

Richard Cloward (1926–) and Lloyd Ohlin (1918–) extended Merton's and Cohen's formulations of anomie theory by suggesting that not all gang delinquents adapt to anomie in the same way. They have differential opportunities, both legitimate and illegitimate. Cloward and Ohlin argue that the type of adaptation made by juvenile gang members depends on the *illegitimate opportunity structure* available to them.[94] They identified three delinquent subcultures or gang types: the criminal, the violent, and the retreatist.[95] According to Cloward and Ohlin, if illegitimate opportunity is available to them, most delinquents will form criminal gangs to make money. However, if neither illegitimate nor legitimate opportunities to make money are available, delinquents often become frustrated and dissatisfied and form violent gangs to vent their anger. Delinquents who adapt in this way probably were the nonutilitarian, malicious, and negativistic ones discussed by Cohen. Finally, some delinquents, for whatever reason, are unable to adapt by joining either criminal or violent gangs. They fail at both criminal and legal activities. These "double failures" retreat from society, as in Merton's retreatist adaptation, and become alcoholics and drug addicts.

The crime prevention implications of anomie or strain theory are straightforward: reduce aspirations, increase legitimate opportunities, or do both.[96] Increasing legitimate opportunities, already a cornerstone of the black civil rights movement, struck a responsive chord as the 1960s began. Reducing aspirations, however, received little attention because to attempt it would be tantamount to rejecting the "American dream," a principal source of motivation in a capitalist society.

When Robert Kennedy was attorney general of the United States under his brother, President John F. Kennedy, he read and was impressed by Cloward and Ohlin's book *Delinquency and Opportunity: A Theory of Delinquent Gangs* (1960). Kennedy was so impressed that he asked Ohlin to help shape a new federal policy on juvenile delinquency.[97] That effort produced the Juvenile Delinquency Prevention and Control Act of 1961.[98] The act included a comprehensive action program developed by Cloward and Ohlin to provide employment opportunities and work training, in combination with community organization and improved social services, to disadvantaged youths and their families.[99] The program was modeled after another effort begun by Cloward and Ohlin in the late 1950s in New York City called Mobilization for Youth.[100] Later the national program was expanded to include all members of the lower class, and when Lyndon Johnson assumed the presidency after

Kennedy's assassination, the program became the foundation of Johnson's War on Poverty.[101]

During the early 1960s, billions of dollars were spent to implement the program and to extend legitimate opportunities. Some of the best known products of the program were the Peace Corps, the Jobs Corps, the Comprehensive Employee Training Act (CETA), and Project Head Start.[102] However, the most tangible result of the effort was a tremendous backlash to what political conservatives argued was an ill-conceived effort to expand the welfare bureaucracy.[103] When Richard Nixon assumed the presidency, the program was discontinued because it had failed to achieve its goals.[104]

The failure of the program does not necessarily invalidate anomie or strain theory or its crime prevention implications because, in actuality, the program was never given a fair opportunity to succeed. It encountered massive resistance from the beginning.[105] However, based on the discouraging results of many other subsequent educational and vocational training programs for delinquent youths, the program may have failed anyway even under the best of circumstances.[106]

Davis's assessment of the "opportunity programs" is even harsher. She argues that (1) morally, they functioned to promote negative stereotypes that blamed the victim; (2) economically, they functioned to funnel the poor into dead-end jobs that maintained "the underclass as a marginal labor force, to the advantage of employers"; and (3) politically, they maintained the status quo by controlling social unrest.[107] What the opportunity programs did not do was grant political power or provide financial resources.[108]

A criticism of the anomie theories of Merton, Cohen, and Cloward and Ohlin is that they have a middle-class bias.[109] In other words, the theories assume that members of the lower class really want to be middle class and that crime and delinquency among lower-class individuals are reactions to their failure to achieve middle-class goals. Walter B. Miller (1933–) was one of those critics. Miller rejected the idea that a delinquent subculture arose through a conflict with middle-class culture. Instead, he argued that the lower class has "a long-established, distinctively patterned tradition with an integrity of its own."[110] Delinquent gangs, in Miller's view, were natural products of the values, or what he called the "focal concerns," of lower-class culture: trouble (the ability to handle it), toughness (physical and emotional strength), smartness (street savvy), excitement (ways that an otherwise drab existence is enlivened), fate (the belief that life outcomes are a matter of luck or chance), and autonomy (being independent of authority figures such as parents, teachers, or the police). Delinquency was "normal" behavior of lower-class youths simply defined as delinquent by the middle and upper classes. In short, for Miller, members of the lower class no more wanted to be middle class than members of the middle class wanted to be lower class.[111]

Perhaps the major problem with "cultural deviance" theories, such as Miller's, is explaining lower-class nondelinquency. Miller accomplishes the feat, and in doing so substantially alters his theory, by attributing lower-class delinquency to individuals or groups who deviate from lower-class culture or who are part of lower-class cultural subtypes.[112] If this were the case, however, then how can lower-class delinquency, or perhaps more accurately, lower-class behavior defined as delinquent by the middle and upper classes, be a product of lower-class culture?

Another major problem with Miller's theory is that no evidence, besides his own, supports it. Every other study, besides Miller's, shows that, "at the very least, overwhelming numbers of the poor give allegiance to the values and principles of the dominant American culture."[113] Additionally, there is no "evidence whatever that the poor perceive their way of life as good and preferable to that of other ways of life."[114] Besides, even if lower-class culture were characterized by Miller's focal concerns, those focal concerns are not necessarily related to delinquency.[115]

Thus, although there may not, in fact, be a middle-class bias to the anomie theories of Merton, Cohen, and Cloward and Ohlin, those theories present other problems. For example, because of their reliance on official statistics, anomie theories focus on lower-class crime and delinquency and ignore white-collar and government crimes.[116] This need not be the case, however. First, Merton maintained that strain could affect people in all social classes. Second, Merton's theory could be applied to white-collar crimes by emphasizing the elasticity of the American dream.[117] That is, when has a person achieved great material wealth? Even wealthy people could experience strain because they have not realized their own expectations about achieving wealth. The insider stock trading crimes of the 1980s are an apt example.

Merton's theory suffers from the problem of overprediction. That is, if strain is caused by the inability to achieve the American dream and is as widespread as Merton implies, then there ought to be much more crime than actually occurs.[118] Merton failed to mention that many potential innovators conform because they lack the opportunity, intelligence, or skills to commit crimes.[119] Potential innovators may also conform if their strain is eased by social supports, an important intervening factor neglected by Merton.[120] (See Chapter 5, the section on humanistic psychological theory, for a description of the concept of social supports.)

A related criticism is that anomie or strain theories ignore individual differences in the understanding of criminal behavior.[121] For example, Merton is charged with assuming that pursuit of the American dream "is a cultural imperative that cuts across class strata, groups, and interests."[122] As such, the theory does not adequately explain gender differences in crime, for example. Merton's theory has also been accused of failing to explain why people choose particular crimes to commit, or why people commit violent and other senseless acts.[123]

Research has also failed to uncover major discrepancies between the aspirations and expectations of delinquents—a necessary component in the production of strain. Delinquents appear to be low on both.[124] However, this problem may stem from another problem, especially in Cloward and Ohlin's version of the theory. The problem is the lack of clarity of such key concepts as aspirations, opportunity, and delinquent subculture.[125] Another related criticism is that the existence of the specific delinquent subcultures or gang types postulated by Cloward and Ohlin is not supported by research.[126] Critics argue that delinquent gang members seldom specialize in particular delinquent activities. Critics also point out that delinquencies are seldom committed by gangs, but instead are committed by a few companions, usually one or two.[127]

In Merton's version of the theory, enormously complex phenomena like culture and social structure are greatly simplified and treated only as abstractions.[128] One may wonder, for example, how prevalent among the public is the "American dream," as defined by Merton?[129] Other strain theorists emphasize other cultural goals besides the "American dream," a point apparently recognized by Merton,[130] and some strain theorists distinguish between short-term and long-term goals. Kornhauser suggests that strain may be a product of frustration in achieving either universal human needs, such as those described by Maslow, or socially induced needs, such as Merton's "American dream."[131] Kornhauser also argues that Merton's distinction between goals and means is arbitrary and misleading. For example, honesty, truth, or even the accumulation of great material wealth can be both a means and a goal.[132]

In a revised version of strain theory, Robert Agnew (1953–) argues that people may not be as goal directed or as conscious of their goals as Merton suggests.[133] According to Agnew, instead of pursuing specific goals, such as monetary success or the American dream, most people are more interested in being treated fairly and justly in whatever activities they pursue.[134] Thus, some people may conclude that based on their own, limited efforts, and compared especially to other people they know, a more limited outcome (for example, a "comfortable" standard of living) may be entirely fair and just.[135] Agnew, by integrating learning theory propositions and recasting anomie theory in social-psychological terms, also identifies additional sources of strain. For example, children who cannot escape abusive parents or an insulting teacher may experience strain.[136] A related criticism is that many more types of adaptation to anomie are possible than the five conceptualized by Merton—perhaps as many as fourteen.[137]

Merton also can be criticized for failing to address the political and economic sources of cultural goals and the social structure that promotes anomie in the first place. Davis, for example, faults Merton for failing to recognize that the myth that "everyone can make it if he [or she] tries" probably is only a "rhetorical device that has the political utility for keeping the 'masses' in their place."[138] In short, Merton can be criticized for not being radical enough in his analysis.

Each of the theories ignores the criminalization process. That is, they fail to consider why or how some harmful and destructive behaviors are defined as criminal, while similar harmful and destructive behaviors are not. Strain theories also fail to consider the effect that social control has on delinquency[139]—a major emphasis of labeling theory (to be discussed later).

Merton and Cohen stressed the anomie of "failure." What about the anomie of "success" (an event Durkheim anticipated) as experienced, for example, by the overnight superstar who is unable to cope with his or her newfound fame?[140] Each of the theories is based on circular reasoning. In other words, anomie is the cause of crime and delinquency, and crime and delinquency are indicators of anomie. Finally, the theories fail to explain why most delinquents, in gangs or otherwise, reform or abstain from criminality when they become adults, especially when social conditions remain relatively the same.[141]

LEARNING THEORIES

Gabriel Tarde (1843–1904) was one of the first theorists to believe that crime was something learned by normal people as they adapted to other people and the conditions of their environment. His theory was a product of his experience as a French lawyer and magistrate and was described in his book *Penal Philosophy*, published in 1890.[142] Because he did not believe that criminals were unique, either physically or psychologically, Tarde completely rejected Lombroso's conception of the born criminal. "Perhaps one is born vicious," he wrote, "but it is quite certain that one becomes a criminal."[143]

For Tarde, becoming a criminal is a learning process, and learning is a social phenomenon. Reflecting the state of knowledge about the learning process in his day, Tarde viewed all social phenomena as the product of imitation. Through *imitation* or *modeling*, a person can learn new responses, such as criminal behavior, by observing others, without performing any overt act or receiving direct reinforcement or reward.[144] Although Tarde did not discuss it, behavior can also be learned by imitating symbolic models where verbal or written instructions are presented. Written instructions include such things as technical manuals; pictorial models include movies, television, and other audiovisual means. In short, for Tarde, criminal behavior is learned by observing and imitating the criminal behavior of other people, something Tarde believed was more likely in urban areas.[145]

The first twentieth-century criminologist to forcefully argue that criminal behavior was learned was Edwin H. Sutherland (1883–1950). His *theory of differential association* developed over thirteen years, between 1934 and 1947,[146] and, together with its more recent modifications, remains one of the most influential theories of crime causation today. The theory explains both differences in crime rates and individual criminal behavior—though the former has been largely ignored.[147] In his text, Sutherland lists the nine propositions of his theory with accompanying commentary:[148]

1. Criminal behavior is learned. Negatively, this means that criminal behavior is not inherited, as such; also, the person who is not already trained in crime does not invent criminal behavior, just as a person does not make mechanical inventions unless he has had training in mechanics.

2. Criminal behavior is learned in interaction with other persons in a process of communication. This communication is verbal in many respects but includes also the "communication of gestures."

3. The principal part of the learning of criminal behavior occurs within intimate personal groups. Negatively, this means that the impersonal agencies of communication, such as movies and newspapers, play a relatively unimportant part in the genesis of criminal behavior.

4. When criminal behavior is learned, the learning includes (a) techniques of committing the crime, which are sometimes very complicated, sometimes very simple; (b) the specific direction of motives, drives, rationalizations, and attitudes.

5. The specific direction of motives and drives is learned from definitions of the legal codes as favorable and unfavorable. In some

societies an individual is surrounded by persons who invariably define the legal codes as rules to be observed, while in others he is surrounded by persons whose definitions are favorable to the violation of the legal codes. In our American society these definitions are almost always mixed, with the consequence that we have culture conflict in relation to the legal codes.

6. A person becomes delinquent because of an excess of definitions favorable to violation of law over definitions unfavorable to violation of law. This is the principle of differential association. It refers to both criminal and anticriminal associations and has to do with counteracting forces. When persons become criminal, they do so because of contacts with criminal patterns and also because of isolation from anticriminal patterns. Any person inevitably assimilates the surrounding culture unless other patterns are in conflict; a southerner does not pronounce r because other southerners do not pronounce r. Negatively, this proposition of differential association means that associations which are neutral so far as crime is concerned have little or no effect on the genesis of criminal behavior. Much of the experience of a person is neutral in this sense, e.g., learning to brush one's teeth. This behavior has no negative or positive effect on criminal behavior except as it may be related to associations which are concerned with the legal codes. This neutral behavior is important especially as an occupier of the time of a child so that he is not in contact with criminal behavior during the time he is so engaged in the neutral behavior.

7. Differential associations may vary in frequency, duration, priority, and intensity. This means that associations with criminal behavior and also associations with anticriminal behavior vary in those respects. "Frequency" and "duration" as modalities of associations are obvious and need no explanation. "Priority" is assumed to be important in the sense that lawful behavior developed in early childhood may persist throughout life, and also that delinquent behavior developed in early childhood may persist throughout life. This tendency, however, has not been adequately demonstrated, and priority seems to be important principally through its selective influence. "Intensity" is not precisely defined, but it has to do with such things as the prestige of the source of a criminal or anticriminal pattern and with emotional reactions related to the associations. In a precise description of the criminal behavior of a person, these modalities would be related in quantitative form and a mathematical ratio be reached. A formula in this sense

has not been developed, and the development of such a formula would be extremely difficult.

8. The process of learning criminal behavior by association with criminal and anticriminal patterns involves all of the mechanisms that are involved in any other learning. Negatively, this means that the learning of criminal behavior is not restricted to the process of imitation. A person who is seduced, for instance, learns criminal behavior by association, but this process would not ordinarily be described as imitation.

9. While criminal behavior is an expression of general needs and values, it is not explained by those general needs and values, since noncriminal behavior is an expression of the same needs and values. Thieves generally steal in order to secure money, but likewise honest laborers work in order to secure money. The attempts by many scholars to explain criminal behavior by general drives and values, such as the happiness principle, striving for social status, the money motive, or frustration, have been, and must continue to be, futile, since they explain lawful behavior as completely as they explain criminal behavior. They are similar to respiration, which is necessary for any behavior, but which does not differentiate criminal from noncriminal behavior.

Modifying a premise from the theory of the Chicago School, Sutherland maintained that differential associations would not produce criminality if it were not for *differential social organization*.[149] In other words, the degree to which communities promote or inhibit criminal associations varies with the way or the degree to which they are organized (that is, the extent of culture conflict).[150]

Though Sutherland's theory has generated a considerable amount of research and is able to explain a wide variety of crimes, including so-called white-collar crimes—a concept Sutherland created, it has been criticized for being untestable.[151] For example, Curran and Renzetti ask, "How can 'an excess of definitions favorable to law violation' be measured or observed?"[152] Even if such definitions could be measured and observed, one critic wonders where an excess of definitions favorable to law violation could be found.[153] As the Chicago theorists Shaw and McKay noted, even in the worst neighborhoods, most residents are law-abiding and subscribe to conventional values. Even residents who do commit crimes generally endorse conventional values much of the time. Furthermore, it is not clear whether differential associations cause crime or are a result of crime.[154] For that matter, it is not clear whether differential associations cause crime at all. If differential associations are so important, then how is the criminal behavior of the recluse Ted Kaczynski—the so-called Unabomber—explained?[155] Even if differential associations are important for most crime, Sutherland's theory has been charged with ignoring individual differences in the ways people respond to procriminal definitions.[156]

Sutherland also has been criticized for underemphasizing the importance of the media in crime causation.[157] Sutherland maintained that "the impersonal agencies of communication, such as movies and newspapers, play a relatively unimportant part." Finally, Sutherland has been criticized for his rather simplistic conception of the learning process.[158]

Regarding the latter criticism, modifications and additions have been made to Sutherland's theory since its final formulation in 1947, as new developments in learning theory have emerged. For example, Daniel Glaser (1918–) modified Sutherland's theory by introducing role theory and by arguing that criminal behavior could be learned by identifying with criminal roles and not just by associating with criminals.[159] Thus, a person could imitate the behavior of a drug dealer without actually having met one. Glaser obviously believed that the media had a greater influence on the learning of criminal behavior than Sutherland believed they had.

Robert L. Burgess (1931–) and Ronald L. Akers (1939–), as well as C. Ray Jeffery (1921–), adapted the principles of operant conditioning and behavior modification, developed by the psychologist B. F. Skinner (1904–1990), and the principles of modeling, as developed by Albert Bandura (1925–), to the explanation of criminal behavior. The first three theorists integrated psychological concepts with sociological ones. Burgess and Akers call their reformulation of Sutherland's theory *differential association–reinforcement theory*, and in a later elaboration, Akers calls it *social learning theory*.[160] Jeffery calls his interpretation the *theory of differential reinforcement*.[161] More recent applications of modern behavioral psychology to an understanding of criminality are found in the works of Wilson and Herrnstein, Akers, and Andrews and Bonta.[162] In the following discussion, the more general term *learning theory* is used to describe this approach.

Learning theory explains criminal behavior and its prevention with the concepts of positive reinforcement, negative reinforcement, extinction, punishment, and modeling or imitation.[163] In learning theory, crime is committed because it is positively reinforced, negatively reinforced, or imitated. The imitation or modeling of criminal behavior already has been described in the earlier discussion of Tarde. Here the focus is on the other concepts.[164]

Positive reinforcement is the presentation of a stimulus that increases or maintains a response. The stimulus, or *reward*, can be either material, such as money, or psychological, such as pleasure.[165] People steal (a response), for example, because of the rewards—for example, the objects or money—that they receive. They use drugs (at least at first) because of the rewards—for example, the pleasure—that the drugs give them.

Negative reinforcement is the removal or reduction of a stimulus whose removal or reduction increases or maintains a response. The stimulus in negative reinforcement is referred to as an *aversive stimulus*. Aversive stimuli, for most people, include pain and fear. A person who is negatively reinforced to steal may be stealing to remove or reduce the aversive stimuli of the fear and pain of poverty. Drug addicts are negatively reinforced to continue to use drugs because using them removes or reduces the aversive stimulus of the pain of drug withdrawal. In short, both positive and negative reinforcement explain why a behavior, such as crime, is maintained or increases. Both types of reinforcement can simultaneously affect the same behavior. In other words, people may commit crime, in this view, both because they are rewarded for it and because it removes aversive stimuli.

According to learning theory, criminal behavior is reduced through extinction or punishment. It is important to emphasize that learning theory does not promise that crime or any other behavior necessarily can be eliminated by these means, only that it can be reduced. *Extinction* (see endnote 163) is a procedure in which behavior that previously was positively reinforced is no longer reinforced. In other words, the rewards have been removed. Thus, if burglars were to continually come up empty in their quests (that is, not to receive rewards for their efforts), they would most likely no longer continue to burglarize. Similarly, if drug users no longer received rewards such as pleasure from their use of drugs, they would most likely no longer use them (assuming, of course, that they were not addicted and using the drugs for negative reinforcement).

Punishment (which Akers calls "positive punishment") is the presentation of an aversive stimulus to reduce a response. It is the principal method used in the United States and other countries to prevent crime or, at least, reduce it. For example, offenders are imprisoned as punishment for their crimes. A problem is that prisons are also "schools of crime." That is, besides their aversive properties, prisons also provide an environment in which criminal behavior is learned.

As a tool of criminal justice in the United States, punishment is not used effectively in other ways as well. That is, it is not used according to learning theory principles.[166] For example, to employ punishment effectively, escape must be prevented. Escape is a natural reaction to the presentation of an aversive stimulus such as imprisonment. In the United States, the chances of an offender's escaping punishment are great. Probation probably does not always function as an aversive stimulus,[167] and most offenders, especially first-time offenders, are not incarcerated.

To be effective, punishment must be applied consistently and immediately. As for immediacy, the process of criminal justice in the United States generally precludes punishment immediately after a criminal act has been committed. The process is a slow and methodical one. Consistent application of punishment is rare because most criminal offenders are not caught.

In addition, extended periods of punishment should be avoided or the effectiveness of the punishment will be reduced. The United States currently imprisons more of its offenders for longer periods than any other country in the world except Russia, though in many cases inmates actually serve only a fraction of their original sentences.[168] A related issue is that punishment is far less effective when the intensity with which the aversive stimulus is presented is increased gradually than when the stimulus is introduced at full intensity. Prolonged imprisonment is a gradual process of punishment that lacks the full intensity and immediacy of corporal punishment, for example.

To be effective, punishment also must be combined with extinction. That is, the rewards that maintain the behavior must be removed. In the United States, after imprisonment, offenders generally are returned to the environments in which their crimes originally were committed and rewarded.

Finally, for punishment to be effective, it must be combined with the positive reinforcement of alternative, prosocial behaviors and the availability of prosocial models as well.[169] Rarely does this happen. For these reasons, then, the ineffectiveness of punishment in the United States should not be surprising because the way punishment is administered in this country violates most of the principles of learning theory.[170]

In concluding this section on the crime prevention implications of learning theory, it is important to emphasize that for learning theorists, positive reinforcement is a much more effective and preferred method of manipulating behavior than is punishment, because positive reinforcement does not suffer the disadvantages associated with punishment. That point is often overlooked by criminal justice decision makers. Among the disadvantages of punishment are that it causes generalization and negative self-concepts. Offenders frequently come to view themselves as bad instead of viewing only their behaviors as bad. Generalizing the evil people do to their personhood severely hampers efforts at rehabilitation. As noted previously, punishment also causes withdrawal or escape. By punishing offenders, the chances of their avoiding detection and capture the next time they commit criminal acts are increased. Finally, punishment causes aggression.[171] The punishing of offenders, particularly nonviolent ones, may inadvertently be producing violent offenders.

Another problem with learning theory as applied to crime, and especially with Sutherland's theory of differential association, is the problem of overprediction. The theory accounts for too much crime and delinquency and has a hard time explaining exceptions.[172] Regarding the former, if criminality is so rewarding for the poor, for example, why do not more poor people commit it? Perhaps it is because they lack the opportunity, skill, or knowledge to commit it. Those possibilities are ignored in differential association theory.[173] Regarding exceptions, how can two brothers who have been raised in the same environment (have the same associations and are exposed to the same rewards) turn out so differently, with one becoming a gangster and the other one becoming a priest? For that matter, why do people who have been rewarded for law-abiding behavior, such as successful business-people or government officials, still commit crimes?[174] Or why do people continue to commit crimes even though it has caused them much pain and agony?[175]

Reinforcement theory, at least as it is used to explain crime, is based on circular reasoning.[176] By definition, a reinforcing stimulus is one that maintains or increases the probability of a behavior. Thus, it is impossible to determine in advance of observing a subsequent behavior whether any particular stimulus is or is not reinforcing. That may not matter so much because data showing a relationship between imitation or reinforcement and crime is either weak or nonexistent.[177] Another fundamental problem is that if all criminal behavior is learned, and none is invented, then how does criminal behavior begin? What is the source of new types of crime?[178]

Learning theory also ignores the criminalization process. It fails to consider why the normal learned behaviors of some groups are criminalized, whereas the normal learned behaviors of other groups are not.[179] For example, why is marijuana consumption illegal, whereas cigarette or alcohol consumption is not? Learning theory ignores the effect that political and economic power has on the definition of criminal behavior.[180]

Sutherland's differential association theory does not explain why individuals have the associations they have, or why the number of definitions favorable or unfavorable to the violation of the law varies from one social context to another.[181] Reference to differential social organization still begs the question of why or how society is differentially organized. Likewise, learning/reinforcement theories, until recently, ignored the social structural influences on the determination of rewards and aversive stimuli.[182] That is, few stimuli are inherently rewarding or aversive, and what is rewarding in any society at any point in time may not be rewarding, or may even be aversive, in another context or under a different circumstance. In short, what generally gives stimuli rewarding or aversive properties is socially determined.[183]

SOCIAL CONTROL THEORIES

Social control theories address the problems of crime and delinquency from an entirely different perspective than do the preceding theories. The seminal question for social control theorists is not why people commit crime and delinquency but rather why they do not. Why do people conform? In other words, social control theorists expect people to commit crime and delinquency unless they are prevented from doing so. They will commit crime, that is, unless they are properly socialized.[184]

Like many of the other sociological theories of crime causation that have been examined, social control theories, as previously noted, have their origins in the work of Durkheim. Not until the 1950s, however, did social control theories begin to emerge to challenge other, more dominant theories, such as strain and differential association. Among the early social control theorists were Albert J. Reiss (1922–), Jackson Toby (1925–), F. Ivan Nye (1918–), and Walter C. Reckless (1899–1988).[185] However, despite the important contributions of those early theorists, modern social control theory in its most detailed elaboration is attributed to the work of Travis Hirschi (1935–). Hirschi's 1969 book, *Causes of Delinquency*, has had a tremendous influence on current criminological thinking.[186] A unique feature of Hirschi's theory (his is a theory of delinquency and not of adult criminality) is that the data on which the theory is based come from self-report surveys rather than from official police or court records or victimization surveys. The self-report surveys, among other things, asked subjects whether they had committed crimes and other offenses.

As did proponents of earlier social control theories, Hirschi argues that delinquency should be expected if a juvenile is not properly socialized. For Hirschi, proper socialization involves the establishment of a strong moral bond between the juvenile and society. This *bond to society* consists of (1) *attachment* to others, (2) *commitment* to conventional lines of action, (3) *involvement* in conventional activities, and (4) *belief* in the moral order and law. Thus, delinquent behavior is likely to occur if there is (1) inadequate attachment, particularly to parents and school,

(2) inadequate commitment, particularly to educational and occupational success, (3) inadequate involvement in such conventional activities as scouting and sports leagues, and (4) inadequate belief, particularly in the legitimacy and morality of the law. For Hirschi, although all four elements of the bond to society are important (the importance of involvement was not supported by his data, however), the most important and most basic element of the bond is attachment to others.

In a more recent book, Michael Gottfredson (1951–) and Hirschi argue that the primary cause of a variety of deviant behaviors, including many different kinds of crime and delinquency, is ineffective child rearing, which produces people with low self-control.[187] Ineffective child rearers, the authors contend, at minimum, fail to monitor their children's behavior, recognize their children's deviant behavior when it occurs, and punish their children's deviant behavior when it is discovered.[188] Children with low self-control frequently have child rearers with low self-control.[189] Low self-control adversely affects a person's ability to accurately calculate the consequences of his or her actions. Because everyone has a predisposition toward criminality, according to this theory, those persons with low self-control find it more difficult to resist. For Gottfredson and Hirschi, people with low self-control tend to be "impulsive, insensitive, physical (as opposed to mental), risk-taking, short-sighted, and nonverbal."[190]

One of the appealing aspects of Hirschi's social control theory, and Gottfredson and Hirschi's theory, too, is its seemingly commonsensical crime prevention implication. To prevent delinquency, juveniles must be properly socialized; they must develop a strong moral bond to society (or self-control). For Hirschi, the units of social control most important in the establishment of the bond are the family, the school, and the law. Not surprisingly, then, programs based on social control theories include parent training and functional-family therapies that attempt to reduce family conflict through dispute settlement and negotiation, reduce neglect and abuse, teach moderate discipline, and promote positive interactions between parents and children.[191] Group homes and surrogate families have been proposed for children whose families are unsalvageable.[192] Counseling and problem-solving and social skills training have been used with "at-risk" children, especially in school settings.[193]

Although social control theory currently is very influential in the thinking of many criminologists, it has not escaped extensive criticism. Perhaps the major problem, at least for some criminologists, is the theory's assumption that delinquency will occur if not prevented.[194] Some criminologists find it troublesome that the theory rejects altogether the idea of delinquent motivation.[195] The theory also rests on the unrealistic assumption that all people have equal skill and ability to commit crime and delinquency.[196]

Regarding social control theory's neglect of delinquent motivation, Charles Tittle (1939–) has attempted to rectify that problem in his integrated "control balance theory."[197] According to Tittle, the probability that a person will commit delinquency, including specific types of delinquency (his theory is about deviance, which includes crime and delinquency), is primarily a result of the interplay of deviant motivation and control. Control, or the limiting of behavioral options, refers to both the amount of control that a person can exercise and the amount of control to which a person is exposed and that is likely to be exercised (that is, the "control ratio"). For Tittle, delinquency is a means by which "people escape deficits and extend surpluses of control."[198]

Four factors are key to Tittle's theory.[199] First is the predisposition toward delinquent motivation, which varies from person to person and from situation to situation. This predisposition is a function of a desire for autonomy, basic biological and psychological needs, and an unbalanced control ratio.[200] "A desire for autonomy" refers to "escaping control over oneself and exercising more control over the social and physical world than one experiences."[201] Because nearly everyone has a desire for autonomy, as well as basic biological and psychological needs, an imbalance in the control ratio is of paramount importance.[202] The second key factor in the theory is provocation or the situational stimulant of delinquent motivation. Provocations are contextual features and include such things as verbal insults, challenges, or displays of weaknesses.[203] The third and fourth factors are the opportunity to commit delinquency, which is most important in explaining specific types of delinquency, and constraint, which refers to the likelihood that a delinquent behavior will activate restraining responses by others. When these four factors converge in a certain way, delinquency is likely. In general, the greater the control ratio imbalance, the greater the likelihood of delinquency. Differences in the magnitude of control imbalances determine the seriousness of specific types of delinquent behavior. When the amount of control exercised relative to the amount of control experienced is balanced—and the other factors are benign—people are likely to conform.

Among problems with Tittle's control balance theory is the calculation of the control ratio, which varies according to the number and types of relationships. So, for example, a father may have a control surplus in relation to a child, but a control deficit in relation to his employer. Depending on the time or situation a husband and wife, for example, may experience either a control surplus or a control deficit. The problem is how to determine the net control ratio from all of an individual's different relationships. Because (1) the number of a person's relationships is almost limitless, (2) some relationships are more influential than others, and (3) the control ratio in any relationship may vary by time and situation, calculating the net control ratio may turn out to be impossible.

Returning to criticisms of Hirschi and Gottfredson and Hirschi's version of social control theory, the latter has been criticized for under-emphasizing the importance of delinquent associates, which has been found to be strongly related to delinquent behavior.[204]

Social control theory also has been criticized for being a good explanation of only less serious delinquency. It does not explain more serious delinquency or adult criminality very well.[205] Critics claim that self-control theory does not explain many types of white-collar, political, or organized crime that are committed by persons with high levels of self-control.[206]

Regarding serious delinquency, critics point out that Hirschi's survey measure of delinquency consisted of only six "less serious" items: "whether they had stolen anything worth less than $2, stolen anything worth between $2 and $50, stolen anything worth more than $50, taken a car without the owner's permission, damaged or destroyed another person's property, or had beat up or deliberately hurt someone other than a sibling."[207] The theory may not explain adult criminality very well because subjects in Hirschi's study were several thousand San Francisco area junior and senior high school boys. The subjects in most other tests of social control theory have been junior high and high school boys too.[208] A problem with junior high and high school boys as subjects is the reliability and validity of the data. They could have lied on the surveys by either not confessing to what they had done or claiming to have done more than they had—two likely possibilities with boys that age and an inherent problem with self-report crime surveys.

Another problem is social control theory's tacit assumption that a consensus exists in society over moral values.[209] Not only does the theory ignore the existence of pervasive social conflict over moral values, it also fails to consider that society, itself, or at least some aspects of society, may be criminogenic.[210]

Another related problem is that social control theory ignores the criminalization process. It fails to consider why certain harmful and destructive behaviors are defined as crime or delinquency, whereas other similar behaviors are not.

Social control theory may also suffer from the problem of over-prediction. It may predict too much delinquency. Unless society is much more effective in preventing delinquency than authorities and the media would lead one to believe, then there should be much more delinquency than currently is the case.[211] The theory does not explain exceptions well, either. The theory does not allow for delinquency by juveniles who are properly socialized, nor does it allow for conformity by juveniles who are not properly socialized. The theory also has trouble in explaining geographical variations in delinquency (and crime). Are people in one country subject to less social control or do they have less self-control than people in another country? Are there similar differences within countries? Self-control theory has the same problem explaining gender differences in delinquency (and crime). Do females have more self-control than males?

Another problem with social control theory is its trouble with "maturational reform."[212] If juveniles become delinquent because they are not properly socialized (or lack self-control), then why do most delinquents stop their delinquent behaviors in early adulthood and not become criminals as adults? Does effective socialization of those delinquents (or the acquisition of self-control) suddenly occur in young adulthood and continue through the rest of their lives?[213]

A related criticism questions the direction of the purported relationship. In other words, does a weakened bond to society cause delinquency, as Hirschi suggests, or does delinquency produce a weakened bond to society?[214]

Still another problem with social control theory is that it does not explain how juveniles are socialized.[215] For example, how are attachments to others produced and changed?

Perhaps the most difficult question for social control theorists to answer is how people were socialized in the first place. In other words, if people are expected to commit crimes unless they are properly socialized, then who socialized the first people, or how were they socialized? So far, social control theorists have not provided a satisfactory answer to that question.

STUDY QUESTIONS

The Contributions of Durkheim

1. What is the cause of crime for Durkheim?
2. How would Durkheim prevent crime?
3. What is Durkheim's major contribution to crime (actually, delinquency causation) theory?
4. How does Durkheim's theory of crime compare with theories described in previous chapters?

The Theory of the Chicago School

5. How would the Chicago theorists explain crime?

6. How would the Chicago theorists prevent crime?

7. What are problems with the theory of the Chicago School?

8. What are two derivatives of the theory of the Chicago School? (Describe them.)

9. What are the policy implications of the two derivatives of the theory of the Chicago School?

10. What are problems with the two derivatives of the theory of the Chicago School?

11. How does the theory of the Chicago School and its derivatives compare with theories previously described in this book?

Functionalism

12. How do functionalists explain crime?

13. What are the policy implications of functionalist theory?

14. What are problems with functionalist theory?

15. How does functionalist theory compare with theories described previously in this book?

Anomie or Strain Theory

16. How would Merton explain crime?

17. How would Cohen explain gang delinquency?

18. What contribution did Cloward and Ohlin make to anomie theory?

19. What contribution did Miller make to anomie theory?

20. How would anomie theorists prevent crime?

21. What are problems with anomie theories?

22. How do anomie theories compare with theories described previously in this book?

Learning Theories

23. How would Tarde explain crime?

24. How would Sutherland explain crime?

25. What modification to Sutherland's theory did Glaser make?

26. How would Burgess and Akers and Jeffery explain crime?   '

27. How would learning theorists prevent crime?

28. What are problems with learning theories of crime?

29. How does learning theory compare with theories described previously in this book?

Social Control Theories

30. How do social control theorists explain delinquency?

31. How would social control theorists prevent delinquency?

32. What are problems with social control theories?

33. How do social control theories compare with theories described previously in this book?

NOTES

1. However, unlike positivists in general, Taylor et al. (1974:87) argue that Durkheim rejected the idea that society is based on a value consensus. Instead, they maintain that, for Durkheim, society, at least under a forced division of labor, is characterized by conflict over moral values.

2. Martin et al. (1990:48).

3. See Vold and Bernard (1986:144).

4. Durkheim (1964:103).

5. Durkheim (1964:3, 123); also see Taylor et al. (1974:69).

6. Durkheim (1964:10, 13); also see Taylor et al. (1974:69).

7. Durkheim (1964:67); also see Taylor et al. (1974:78). Beirne and Messerschmidt (2000:94) observe that, "for Durkheim . . . social phenomena (such as law and crime) have an objective existence of their own and exist quite independently of the individuals who experience them."

8. See Durkheim (1964:70).

9. Taylor et al. (1974:79).

10. See Vold and Bernard (1986:147–148).

11. Durkheim (1964:71); also see Taylor et al. (1974:80). Although Durkheim identifies functions of crime and argues that it is a normal aspect of society, he did not want to be known as an apologist for it. He noted that even though crime is a social fact, we must still abhor it (Durkheim, 1964:72, fn. 13).

12. Durkheim (1933:375); also see Taylor et al. (1974:75).

13. Durkheim (1933:79); also see Taylor et al. (1974:77).

14. See Taylor et al. (1974:77, 85, 87).

15. Durkheim (1933:377).

16. Durkheim (1933:278–279, 378); also see Taylor et al. (1974:77–78, 87–88). Taylor et al. maintain that Durkheim, unlike Comte, was a

radical in his politics and approach to social order.

17. Many of the sociological theories are theories of delinquency and not of adult criminality.

18. Vold and Bernard (1986:160).

19. See Vold and Bernard (1986:160).

20. See Vold and Bernard (1986:161); Davis (1975:46).

21. Vold and Bernard (1986:161).

22. Park et al. (1928).

23. See Vold and Bernard (1986:163–164).

24. Much of the material in this section is from Shaw (1929); Shaw and McKay (1931, 1942); and, especially, Vold and Bernard (1986:165–171).

25. See Shaw (1930, 1931, 1938).

26. See Vold and Bernard (1986:171). In a test of social disorganization theory, Sampson and Groves (1989), following the original conceptualization of Shaw and McKay, employed the following five indicators of social disorganization: (1) residents of low economic status, (2) many different ethnic groups, (3) a high frequency of residential turnover, (4) dysfunctional families, and (5) urbanization.

27. See Vold and Bernard (1986:171–172). Shaw and his colleagues believed that delinquency was culturally transmitted (hence, this part of the theory is sometimes referred to as cultural transmission theory; see Williams and McShane, 1994:55). Kornhauser (1978:62) claims that within Shaw and McKay's theory is a distinct social control theory of delinquency that has been "blurred" by their "merging it with a cultural deviance [theory] in which they emphasized the 'cultural transmission' of delinquency by the delinquent gang." Social control theory is examined in a later section of this chapter.

28. Vold and Bernard (1986:180).

29. See Vold and Bernard (1986:180–181).

30. Vold and Bernard (1986:181).

31. Vold and Bernard (1986:181); but see National Institute (1977:28) and Schlossman et al. (1984:46) for a different view.

32. See, for example, Wilson (1987).

33. See Vold and Bernard (1986:181–182); Einstadter and Henry (1995:142).

34. See Curran and Renzetti (1994:141–142); Vold and Bernard (1986:181–182); Einstadter and Henry (1995:142).

35. See Mills (1942).

36. See Suttles (1968).

37. See Matza (1969:48).

38. See Vold and Bernard (1986:174–175); Davis (1975:41–51); Katz (1988).

39. See Davis (1975:49).

40. See Einstadter and Henry (1995:134).

41. Tittle (1995:2)

42. See Curran and Renzetti (1994:142); Vold and Bernard (1986:173–174); Einstadter and Henry (1995:140–141).

43. See Taylor et al. (1974:125); Einstadter and Henry (1995:140).

44. Babbie (1992:96); Andrews and Bonta (1994:12–16).

45. See Wilson and Herrnstein (1985:290); Vold and Bernard (1986:176).

46. Newman (1976, originally published in 1972). Also see Jeffery (1977) and Brantingham and Brantingham (1991) for extensions of Newman's theory. For other recent extensions of ecological theory, see

Brantingham and Brantingham (1984); Bursik (1984); Stark (1987); Vila (1994).

47. See Williams and McShane (1994:61).

48. Cisneros (1995:3).

49. Cisneros (1995:23).

50. Wilson and Herrnstein (1985:309).

51. Cohen and Felson (1979).

52. Cohen and Felson (1979).

53. Cohen and Felson (1979).

54. Cohen and Felson (1979).

55. An extended discussion of this problem can be found in the section on social control theories presented later in this chapter.

56. Tittle (1995:14).

57. Tittle (1995:15).

58. See Einstadter and Henry (1995:70).

59. See Einstadter and Henry (1995:71).

60. See Davis (1975:65).

61. Davis (1975:65–66).

62. Davis (1975:66).

63. See Davis (1975:74, 92); also see Gouldner (1971).

64. Davis (1975:80–81, 92).

65. See Davis (1975:82).

66. Davis (1971); also see Davis (1975:81–82).

67. See Davis (1975:82–85).

68. Cited in Taylor et al. (1974:210–211).

69. See Durkheim (1964:66); also see Davis (1975:71–72, 88–89).

70. See Davis (1975:91).

71. See Davis, (1975:68, 92).

72. See Davis (1975:67).

73. See Davis (1975:67, 90).

74. See Davis (1975:72–73).

75. See Davis (1975:67).

76. See Davis (1975:68, 81, 90–92).

77. See Davis (1975:96).

78. Martin et al. (1990:212).

79. See Messner and Rosenfeld (1994) for a contemporary version of the theory. They integrate anomie theory with social control theory and radical theory, though radical theory propositions may have been unintended.

80. Vold and Bernard (1986:186–187).

81. Vold and Bernard (1986:187).

82. Merton (1938).

83. But see Taylor et al. (1974:98) for another view.

84. Vold and Bernard (1986:193).

85. Cohen's theory of gang delinquency, as well as Cloward and Ohlin's theory of differential opportunity (to be discussed shortly), has been considered a subcultural theory rather than, or in addition to, an anomie or strain theory (see Williams and McShane, 1994:105). Cohen was the first criminologist to apply the concept of subculture to the study of delinquency (Beirne and Messerschmidt, 2000:147).

86. Cohen (1955:25); also see Vold and Bernard (1986:194).

87. Cohen (1955:30–31).

88. Cohen (1955:65–66, 136); also see Vold and Bernard (1986:194).

89. Actually, for Cohen, status frustration was a problem only for working-class juveniles. For middle-class juveniles, on the other hand, delinquency was primarily a way of coping with a basic anxiety in the

area of sex role identification (Cohen, 1955:164–169).

90. Cohen (1955:84–93).

91. Cohen (1955:28, 112–119, 133); also see Vold and Bernard (1986:195).

92. Cohen (1955:134–135); also see Vold and Bernard (1986:195).

93. Cohen (1955:37); also see Vold and Bernard (1986:195).

94. Cloward and Ohlin (1960:148).

95. Cloward and Ohlin (1960:Chap. 7); also see Vold and Bernard (1986:197).

96. See Taylor et al. (1974:94); Schur (1969:230–232).

97. Vold and Bernard (1986:201).

98. Vold and Bernard (1986:201).

99. Vold and Bernard (1986:201).

100. Curran and Renzetti (1994:169).

101. Curran and Renzetti (1994:169); Vold and Bernard (1986:201).

102. Williams and McShane (1994:121).

103. Vold and Bernard (1986:201–202).

104. Vold and Bernard (1986:201).

105. Curran and Renzetti (1994:169); Vold and Bernard (1986:201).

106. See Wilson and Herrnstein (1985:335) on vocational training programs; also see Vold (1979:223).

107. Davis (1975:118).

108. Davis (1975:118).

109. See Vold (1979:223).

110. Miller (1958).

111. See Vold (1979:224).

112. Kornhauser (1978:205); also see Costello (1997).

113. Ryan (1976:134); also see Kornhauser (1978:206–207).

114. Ryan (1976:134); also see Kornhauser (1978:208).

115. Kornhauser (1978:208).

116. See Curran and Renzetti (1994:152, 164); Vold (1979:226); Taylor et al. (1974:106–107).

117. See, for example, Friedrichs (1996:232).

118. See Taylor et al. (1974:107); Kornhauser (1978:148).

119. Tittle (1995:5).

120. Cullen and Wright (1997).

121. See Andrews and Bonta (1994:95–96).

122. Davis (1975:102).

123. Lanier and Henry (1998:234); Tittle (1995:2).

124. Martin et al. (1990:284–285); Kornhauser (1978:180).

125. Martin et al. (1990:286–288).

126. Martin et al. (1990:288); Kornhauser (1978:159–160).

127. See Kornhauser (1978:243).

128. See Davis (1975:104).

129. Taylor et al. (1974:104–105); Kornhauser (1978:163, 166).

130. Williams and McShane (1994:91). For example, Messner and Rosenfeld (1994) emphasize the American cultural goal of consumption. In later writings, Merton argued that "cultural success goal" could be substituted for money with the same results.

131. Kornhauser (1978:139).

132. Kornhauser (1978:162).

133. Agnew (1992).

134. Agnew (1992).

135. Agnew (1992).

136. Agnew (1985b).

137. Agnew (1992); Dubin (1959).

138. Davis (1975:102); also see Kornhauser (1978:164).

139. See Taylor et al. (1974:108).

140. See Davis (1975:105).

141. See Matza (1964).

142. See Vold and Bernard (1986:208–209).

143. Tarde (1968:256).

144. See Bandura and Walters (1963).

145. Beirne and Messerschmidt (2000:91).

146. See Vold and Bernard (1986:210).

147. Williams and McShane (1994:78).

148. Sutherland and Cressey (1974:75–77).

149. Sutherland and Cressey (1974:77, 89, 93–96); also see Vold and Bernard (1986:213).

150. Sutherland and Cressey (1974:107–109). Because of the importance of the concepts of differential social organization and culture conflict in Sutherland's theory, he is considered a "value-conflict" theorist, albeit an apolitical one, by some (see Davis, 1975:Chap. 6). A political-conflict theory is addressed later in this book.

151. See National Institute (1977:31); Kornhauser (1978:189); Martin et al. (1990:164).

152. Curran and Renzetti (1994:188). However, see Andrews (1980) for an explanation of how they can be measured.

153. Sampson (1999:443–444); but see Akers (1999:478–479).

154. Lanier and Henry (1998:140); but see Akers (1999:479–480) with regard to delinquent peers.

155. Sampson (1999:441).

156. Beirne and Messerschmidt (2000:136); Sampson (1999:446).

157. Curran and Renzetti (1994:190).

158. Curran and Renzetti (1994:190).

159. Glaser (1956).

160. Burgess and Akers (1966); Akers (1985).

161. Jeffery (1965).

162. Wilson and Herrnstein (1985); Akers (1994, 1998); Andrews and Bonta (1994).

163. Note that Akers (1994) and Andrews and Bonta (1994) call extinction negative punishment. However, the concept of extinction will be used here.

164. See Rachlin (1976) for a description of the concepts.

165. In the case of habitual offenders, rewards may also be nonsocial and neurophysiological, see Wood et al. (1997).

166. See Jeffery (1977:274–276).

167. This is one reason why so-called intermediate punishments, such as intensive supervision probation and parole, home confinement and electronic monitoring, and day reporting centers have been introduced.

168. Inmates likely will be serving more of their original sentences because of recent legislation requiring, for certain offenses, mandatory minimum sentences, serving 85 percent (or some other fraction) of the original sentence, and a sentence of life imprisonment upon conviction of a third felony ("three strikes and you're out"). The abolition of parole in some jurisdictions will also add to the amount of time actually served by prison inmates.

169. See Bandura and Walters (1963:212); Andrews and Bonta (1994:202–205).

170. Wilson and Herrnstein (1985:229–230) maintain that "problem" or "antisocial" children also are a product of ineffective punishment by parents.

171. See Jeffery (1977:275).

172. See Martin et al. (1990:165).

173. Tittle (1995:3).

174. Lanier and Henry (1998:144); Sampson (1999:447); Tittle (1995:111); but see Akers (1998:98–101).

175. Tittle (1995:111).

176. See Krohn (1999:470); Tittle (1995:111).

177. Sampson (1999:443).

178. Glueck (1956); Costello (1997); but see Matsueda (1997).

179. Vold and Bernard (1986:229–230).

180. But see Vold and Bernard (1986:226) for a different view.

181. Tittle (1995:3).

182. See Akers (1998). Akers does not present a fully articulated integrated theory. Rather, he simply states that certain social structural factors, primarily drawn from anomie, social disorganization, and conflict theories, affect social psychological processes— that is, social learning concepts, which in turn influence both criminal behavior and crime rates. But which social structural factors are most important? Akers only tells us that the social structural factors strongly related to crime rates will also be strongly related to social learning concepts, and those social structural factors not strongly related to crime rates will not be strongly related to social learning concepts (1998:336). He admits that his theory "does not attempt to explain why a society has the [social structural factors, such as] culture, age structure, class system, race system, family system, economic system, gender/sex role system, or religious system that it has" (1998:336). Nor, for that matter, does his theory, as he again concedes, "explain (by reference to history, social change, or other macro-level variables) why there is social disorganization, conflict, or inequality in society" (1998:336).

183. See the discussion of interactionism in Chapter 7.

184. Lanier and Henry (1998:158) observe that social control theories provide the "missing half" of Sutherland's theory of differential association and other learning theories by suggesting that law-abiding behaviors are learned through a process of socialization. Sutherland's focus was on the learning of law-violating behaviors.

185. See Reiss (1951); Toby (1957); Nye (1958); Reckless (1961).

186. See Hirschi (1969).

187. Gottfredson and Hirschi (1990).

188. Gottfredson and Hirschi (1990:97).

189. Gottfredson and Hirschi (1990:100–101).

190. Gottfredson and Hirschi (1990:90).

191. Lanier and Henry (1998:166).

192. Lanier and Henry (1998:166).

193. Lanier and Henry (1998:166).

194. As noted in Chapter 1, the seventeenth-century English philosopher Thomas Hobbes believed that all human beings are basically evil and, therefore, likely to commit crime. This idea may have been derived from the Christian belief that everyone is born into original sin. Similar ideas about human nature are found in Freudian psychoanalytic theory, which is considered a prototype for

control theories. In Freud's version of psychoanalytic theory, it is assumed that everyone is capable of committing crime because of the sexual and aggressive drives of the id (see Andrews and Bonta, 1994:70; Kornhauser, 1978:142). Note, however, that Hirschi is one control theorist who does not believe it is necessary to explain criminal behavior as the result of an uncontrolled id (see Andrews and Bonta, 1994:83). Early social control theorists assumed that all human beings were frustrated in the attempt to satisfy their needs or wants, given scarcity of means, and that need frustration was a "chronic condition of humanity" (see Kornhauser, 1978:47). Criminal behavior is one likely outcome of this chronic condition. Other theorists suggest that control theories do not need to assume that people are basically bad. For them, it is only necessary to assume at least a neutral human nature (see Williams and McShane, 1994:181).

195. National Institute (1977:44). Social control theorists do not actually deny delinquent motivation. They only deny a special motivation such as social disorganization or anomie. They assume that individuals are motivated to commit delinquency because of their human nature (but see Williams and McShane, 1994:181, for a different view).

196. Tittle (1995:59).

197. Tittle (1995).

198. Tittle (1995:142).

199. Tittle (1995:142).

200. Tittle (1995:147–148).

201. Tittle (1995:145).

202. Tittle (1995:148).

203. Tittle (1995:163).

204. Andrews and Bonta (1994:84).

205. Martin et al. (1990:200); Agnew (1985a).

206. Beirne and Messerschmidt (2000:221); Gottfredson and Hirschi disagree.

207. Curran and Renzetti (1994:200).

208. See Curran and Renzetti (1994:210–212).

209. National Institute (1977:43–44).

210. See Schur (1969).

211. Perhaps there is as much delinquency as social control theory predicts, but because most delinquency goes undiscovered and unreported, there is no way of knowing.

212. National Institute (1977:43).

213. See Einstadter and Henry (1995:196) and Williams and McShane (1994:192–193) for an affirmative response to this question.

214. Agnew (1985a); Liska and Reed (1985).

215. National Institute (1977:43).

7

⌗

Critical Theories

Interactionism and Labeling Theory

Conflict Theory

Radical Theory

Other Critical Theories
British or Left Realism
Peacemaking Criminology
Feminism
Postmodernism and Poststructuralism

Critical theories are, in part, a product of the demystification of American society that began toward the end of the 1950s. *Demystification* is the correcting of misconceptions or "setting the record straight." At that time, a small group of social scientists began to question the activities and priorities of the U.S. government and major American corporations, as well as the functionalist theory that often served as a justification. This questioning and skepticism was due to the revelation about how the American public was being misled about the "true" nature of current events, and about how the interests of the power elite were being served by those actions.[1]

In the political arena, the public's eyes were being opened to McCarthyism, the Bay of Pigs, the Cuban missile crisis, political and racial assassination, the government's abandonment of the civil rights movement, military intervention in Latin America and Asia, the domestic pacification objectives of the War on Poverty, and the destruction of communities for urban renewal. Revelations about corporate misdeeds included price-fixing conspiracies, price gouging, the sale of worthless or dangerous products, deceptive or fraudulent advertising, unsafe working conditions, and pollution and destruction of the environment. Particularly disturbing was evidence of the complicity of social scientists in some of those unsavory and, in some cases, illegal actions under the guise of a "value-free" social science.[2] During the next decades, disclosures about secret and illegal activities of the U.S. government and major U.S. corporations became commonplace. Concepts like racism, sexism, capitalism, imperialism, monopoly, exploitation, and oppression were being employed with greater frequency to describe the social landscape. In the 1960s, the period of naive acceptance of the status quo and the belief in the purely benevolent actions of government ended for many social scientists, and the seeds of critical theory began to sprout. For critical criminologists, government and corporate crimes highlight structural causes that are not readily apparent when conventional street crime is examined.[3]

Critical theories, for the most part, are sociological theories. However, not surprisingly, the basic assumptions of critical theories differ both from those of classical and neoclassical theories and from those of positivist theories. First, unlike classical and neoclassical theories, which assume that human beings have free will, and positivist theories, which assume that human beings are determined, either in a "hard" or "soft" way, critical theories assume that human beings are both determined *and* determining.[4] In other words, critical theories assume that human beings are the creators of the institutions and structures that ultimately dominate and constrain them. Furthermore, as creators, they are capable of changing institutions and structures.

Second, in contrast to both classical and neoclassical and positivist theories, which assume that society is characterized fundamentally by a consensus over moral values, whether by social contract in the former or the collective conscience or the division of labor in the latter, critical theories assume that conflict is the norm, that society is characterized primarily by conflict over moral values.

Finally, unlike positivist theories that assume that social scientists, including criminologists, can be value-neutral or objective in their work, critical theories assume that such a position is impossible. Critical theorists assume that everything they do is value-laden by virtue of their being human. Many critical theorists believe that the most intellectually honest alternative to the value-neutral stance is to be honest and forthright about one's values and let consumers of one's work evaluate that work in light of an explicitly articulated value position.

Having said this, it is important to note that although many criminologists consider themselves critical, there actually are few critical criminologists.[5] The primary reason is that although most criminologists are typically critical of dissonant theoretical positions, few criminologists, including so-called critical or radical criminologists, are, in the tradition of the Greek philosopher Socrates, critical of their own positions. That is, few criminologists are *reflexive* or self-conscious about their own position.[6] This failure of criminologists to be critical and reflexive about their own theoretical perspectives is one of criminology's major problems.

INTERACTIONISM
AND LABELING THEORY

The focus of interactionist and labeling theory is the *meaning* of crime and criminality.[7] Attention is shifted from the positivist concern with the peculiarities of the criminal actor to the *criminalization process*—the way people and actions are defined as criminal.[8] From this perspective, the distinguishing feature of all "criminals" is that they have been the object of a *negative social reaction*.[9] In other words, they have been designated by the state and its agents as different and "bad."[10]

Interactionism and labeling theory have their roots in the symbolic interactionism of George Herbert Mead (1863–1931), whose ideas on the subject can be summarized in three propositions. First, "human beings act toward things on the basis of the meanings that the things have for them."[11] By this, Mead meant that people often interpret the same event or behavior differently because of the unique meanings that they attach to it.[12] Consider, for example, the Ford Pinto case.[13]

Between 1971 and 1976, Ford Motor Company executives made the decision to sell Ford Pintos (and Mercury Bobcats) to the public, knowing that the placement of the gas tank made the cars susceptible to fiery explosions on rear impact at relatively slow speeds. They also knew that innocent people probably would be killed and injured as a result. Knowing this, they decided that it would be cheaper in the long run to settle the lawsuits initiated by injured drivers and passengers and the families of killed drivers and passengers than to recall the cars and install an $11 metal shield to protect the gas tank. As it turned out, the Ford executives were correct in their belief that people would die and be injured as a result of their decisions. They were wrong, however, in assuming that settling lawsuits would be cheaper than recalling the vehicles and installing the metal shield. In any event, the relevant question for this discussion is whether the Ford executives who made those decisions were guilty of any crimes. Although the courts ultimately decided that they were not, many people believe that they were. The point is that the actions of the Ford executives are interpreted differently by different people, depending on the meaning the event has for them.

Mead's second proposition is that "the meaning of things arises out of the social interaction that one has with one's fellows."[14] By this, Mead meant that meaning resides neither in the thing itself nor exclusively in the sender or the receiver. Meaning is the product of negotiations between the sender, the receiver, and relevant social others.[15] Thus, for example, whether a woman forced to have sexual intercourse against her will has been raped in a legal sense depends on the act's interpretation by police, prosecutors, judges, juries, and especially the woman herself. It may also depend on such things as the amount of resistance offered by the victim, the victim's sexual history, and a host of other factors.

Mead's third proposition is that "these meanings are handled in, and modified through, an interpretative process used by the person in dealing with things he encounters."[16] In other words, in the interpretation of an event, people not only receive meaning but create it as well. Thus, people's actions are, at least to some extent, determined by themselves.[17] This proposition is the basis for the critical theory assumption that people are both determined and determining.[18] For example, when then-Colonel Oliver North diverted funds to the Nicaraguan *contras* in defiance of the Boland Amendment prohibiting such activity, were his acts heroic or criminal? Although the public has mixed feelings about North's actions, there can be little doubt that North himself believes his actions were heroic.

A lesson to be learned from Mead's theory is that one must be careful not to assume that his or her interpretation of a criminal act is the correct one. Even if the interpretation seems logical to that person, the act might be interpreted very differently by the actor or another independent observer.[19] That may be why many criminal acts are committed by people who do not define themselves as criminals.[20] To truly understand a criminal act, then, it is necessary to understand the act from the perspective of the actor, that is, from the actor's definition of self, situation, and society.[21]

According to Mead, self-image, or conception of self, is constructed by a person's interpretation of the way that person believes other people see him or her.[22] Mead called this self-image "the self as a social construct." Charles Cooley (1864–1929) referred to it as "the looking glass self."[23] Thus, for example, if a child believes that other people believe he or she is bad or delinquent, then there is a good chance that he or she will believe it too.

People define their situations by the meanings they negotiate with other people. This may explain why two people can have entirely different conceptions of ostensibly the same environment. For one life is interpreted as rosy; for the other, as hell. This difference of interpretation may resolve the problem of overprediction.

Finally, conceptions of society also are formed through an interpretative process. Whether people view society as wonderful and full of opportunity or horrible and oppressive depends on how they interpret society within the context of their social interactions. For Mead, then, human behavior is explained by the meaning people give to self, situation, and society.

Labeling theory, or the "societal reaction" approach, uses this theoretical framework to explain why people commit crimes and conceive of themselves as criminals. As Howard Becker (1928–) relates, "Social groups create deviance [crime] by making the rules whose infraction constitutes deviance [crime], and by applying those rules to particular people and labeling them as outsiders."[24]

It is important to note that labeling theorists attempt to explain only what Edwin Lemert (1912–1996) called "secondary deviance."[25] For purposes of this discussion, *secondary deviance* is the commission of crime after the first criminal act, with the acceptance of a criminal label. Secondary deviance begins with an initial criminal act, or what Lemert called "primary deviance." The causes of initial criminal acts are unspecified. Nevertheless, if society, especially official agents of the state, reacts negatively to an initial criminal act, the offender will likely be *stigmatized*, or negatively labeled. It is possible, even likely, that an initial criminal act will not be reacted to at all, or that the offender will not accept or internalize the negative label. However, if the negative label is successfully applied to the offender, the label may produce a *self-fulfilling prophecy*—a concept created by Robert Merton[26]—in which the offender's self-image is defined by the label. Secondary deviance is the prophecy fulfilled.

The crime prevention implication of labeling theory is simply not to label or to employ "radical nonintervention."[27] This might be accomplished through decriminalization (the elimination of many behaviors from the scope of the criminal law), diversion (removing offenders from involvement in the criminal justice process), greater due process protections (replacing discretion with the rule of law), and deinstitutionalization (a policy of reducing jail and prison populations and construction).[28]

As is well known, once a person is labeled and stereotyped as a "criminal," he or she probably will be shunned by law-abiding society, have difficulty finding a good job, lose some civil rights (if convicted of a felony), and suffer a variety of other disabilities. The criminal (and delinquent) label is conferred by all of the agencies of criminal justice—the police, the courts, and the correctional apparatus—as well as the media, the schools, churches, and other social institutions. The irony is that in its attempt to reduce crime and delinquency, society inadvertently may be increasing it by labeling people and producing secondary deviance.[29]

A provocative alternative to the nonintervention strategy is John Braithwaite's (1951–) "reintegrative shaming."[30] Reintegrative shaming is a form of restorative justice, an alternative to the punitive justice currently used in the United States and many other countries.[31] The primary goals of restorative justice are to restore the health of the community, repair the harm done, meet victims' needs, and require the offender to contribute to those repairs. In Braithwaite's strategy, disappointment is expressed for the offender's actions, the offender is shamed and punished, but, what is more important, following the expression of disappointment and shame is a concerted effort on the part of the community to forgive the offender and reintegrate him or her back into society. Braithwaite contends that the practice of reintegrative shaming is one of the primary reasons for Japan's relatively low crime rate.[32]

In taking the side of the "underdog"[33] or adopting what Becker called an "unconventional sentimentality,"[34] labeling theorists tended to romanticize the criminal offender as a primitive revolutionary reacting to an unjust society. A problem with such a view is that it ignores the very real harm and suffering caused by those offenders. More times than not, offenders and their victims are from the same social groups. Victimizing members of one's own group hardly can be considered liberating.

Labeling theory also has been criticized for not being a theory at all but rather a "sensitizing perspective."[35] This criticism, moreover, has been acknowledged as valid by some of the social scientists (for example, Howard Becker) whose work is identified with the perspective.[36] The criticism, however, in no way diminishes the contribution of labeling ideas.

Another criticism of labeling theory is that it does not explain primary deviance.[37] Critics point out that the label does not create the criminal behavior in the first place. This criticism seems unfair, however, because labeling theorists are quite clear that the object of their theory is secondary and not primary deviance.

A more legitimate problem with labeling theory is that it tends to overemphasize the importance of the official labeling process.[38] On the one hand, the impression is given that innocent people are arbitrarily stigmatized by an oppressive society and that, as a result, they begin a life of crime.[39] That scenario probably does not happen very often. On the other hand, the impression is given that offenders resist the criminal label and accept it only when they are no longer capable of fighting it.[40] As for the latter, in some communities the label criminal, or some variation of it, is actively sought.[41] In some cases, people develop criminal self-images without ever having been labeled criminal in the first place.[42] Furthermore, if the delinquent label is so stigmatizing, why do most delinquents not engage in adult criminality (the problem of "maturational reform")? For that matter, if the criminal label is so stigmatizing, why do most criminals stop their illegal activities when they reach middle age?[43]

Labeling theory also has been faulted for ignoring individual differences among criminal offenders. For example, critics contend that, whereas radical nonintervention or restorative justice may be appropriate for low-risk cases, it may not be appropriate for higher-risk cases.[44]

A major problem with labeling theory is that it holds a simplistic view of the criminalization process.[45] For example, as Becker maintains, "Social groups create deviance [crime] by making the rules whose infraction constitutes deviance [crime], and by applying those rules to particular people and labeling them as outsiders."[46] But what social groups create crime? What is missing in labeling theory is a coherent conception of the interrelationship of power, the state, and law creation.

Perhaps the most telling problem with labeling theory is the question whether the act of stigmatizing someone as criminal or delinquent causes more crime and delinquency than it prevents.[47] To date, the answer is unknown.

CONFLICT THEORY

Unlike classical or neoclassical and positivist theories, which assume that society is characterized primarily by consensus, conflict theory assumes that society is based primarily on conflict between competing interest groups (for example, the rich against the poor, corporations against labor, whites against minorities, men against women, adults against children, Protestants against Catholics, Democrats against

Republicans). In many cases, competing interest groups are not equal in power and resources, and consequently one group is dominant and the other is subordinate.

Although they did not address crime per se, conflict criminology is based on the seminal ideas of the German sociologists Max Weber (1864–1920) and Georg Simmel (1858–1918), whose "liberal" ideas about social conflict, in large part, were a reaction to the more radical ideas of another German social thinker, Karl Marx (1818–1883). (Marx's contribution to radical criminology is addressed in the next section.) One of the earliest theorists in the United States to apply conflict theory to the study of crime was George B. Vold (1896–1967). For Vold and other conflict theorists, such as Thorstein Sellin (1896–1994), Austin T. Turk (1934–), Richard Quinney (1934–), and William J. Chambliss (1933–), many behaviors are defined as crimes because it is in the interests of dominant groups to do so.[48] As for those behaviors that are in everyone's interest to be defined as criminal, members of dominant groups are frequently able to violate them with impunity because of their control of the state. When they cannot escape punitive action, they usually face a civil remedy for administrative or regulatory agency violations. Prison sentences are rarely imposed. They are also able to evade the most punitive penalties for their crimes by being able to hire the best attorneys. For conflict criminologists, people are only labeled as criminal when it is in the interests of dominant groups to do so; and because it generally is not in the interest of dominant groups to label its own members as criminal, members of subordinate groups are more likely to be stigmatized in that way.

Dominant groups use crime and the criminal law, then, to control subordinates. However, the image that is projected for public consumption is quite different. The public image is that the criminal law and the state that administers it are value-neutral institutions.[49] That is, neither the law nor the state is presumed to have a vested interest in which party to a dispute "wins." The only interest of the state and the law, at least as far as the public image is concerned, is in making sure that disputes between competing interest groups are resolved justly and, what is more important, peacefully. This public image allows dominant groups to create the impression that interests of the two groups are the same. This ploy legitimizes the authority and practices of dominant groups and allows them to surreptitiously achieve their own parochial interests, generally at the expense of other groups. Crime also serves the interests of dominant groups by deflecting the attention of subordinate group members from the exploitation they endure from dominant groups and turning that attention to other subordinate group members defined as criminal.[50]

All behavior, including criminal behavior, in this view, is the result of people acting in ways consistent with their social positions. Whether white-collar crime or ordinary street crime, crime is a response to a person's social situation. The reason members of subordinate groups appear in official criminal statistics more frequently than members of dominant groups is that the latter are better able than the former to ensure that the responses of subordinate group members to their social situations will be defined and reacted to as criminal.[51] For conflict theorists, the amount of crime in a society is a function of the extent of conflict generated by *stratification, hierarchical relationships, power differentials,* or the ability of some groups to dominate other groups in that society. Crime, in short, is caused by *relative powerlessness.*[52]

Conflict theory has two principal crime prevention implications. On the one hand, dominant groups could cede some of their power to subordinate groups, making the latter groups more powerful and reducing conflict.[53] Increasing equality in that way might be accomplished by redistributing wealth through a more progressive taxation scheme, for example. On the other hand, dominant group members could become more effective rulers and subordinate group members better subjects. To do so, dominant groups would have to do a better job of convincing subordinate groups that the current inequitable distribution of power in society is legitimate and in their mutual interests. Members of subordinate groups, in turn, would have to either believe it or resign themselves to their inferior status. Either way, dominant group members hope that over time subordinate group members will learn to follow those who dominate them.

Conflict theory has been criticized by psychologists for ignoring individual differences among criminal offenders.[54] Critics charge that conflict theorists ignore the variation in how people respond to relative powerlessness and the conflict that often results. Conflict theorists fail to explain why criminal offenders choose particular crimes to commit. Ignored in conflict theory are such important factors as the opportunity, intelligence, and skills necessary to commit various crimes.[55]

A related problem is that people, at either the individual or group level, are rarely totally dominated or dominating.[56] At the individual level, people may be dominant in one group (for example, the family) but subordinate in another (for instance, at the workplace). At the group level, people may simultaneously be members of both dominant and subordinate groups. For example, they may be members of a dominant economic or political group but, at the same time, also be members of subordinate religious, racial, or ethnic groups. Furthermore, the status of groups or the status of individuals within groups, as either dominant or subordinate, may change over time.

Conflict theorists may also overestimate the extent of conflict in society over moral values, at least with regard to some types of crime. Numerous studies (albeit older ones) show that the American public, regardless of race or class, almost universally condemns crimes involving theft and violence.[57] Still, while there may be near universal condemnation of crimes such as murder, rape, and robbery, people may nonetheless differ on what they believe constitutes murder, rape, and robbery. For example, were the actions of the Ford Motor Company executives, discussed in the last section, murder? Is euthanasia murder?

Another criticism is that, like positivists, some conflict theorists delude themselves into believing that they can be value-neutral or objective in their work—or at least be able to approximate it.[58] For example, Turk writes:

> Nonpartisan conflict theory and analysis assumes that the ideological bent of theorists or the political utilities of theories are irrelevant for assessing the validity of knowledge claims. . . . Recognizing that values can never be totally excluded from the research process, nonpartisan conflict analysts also recognize that approximations to value-neutral procedures and knowledge are possible.[59]

As noted previously, most critical criminologists believe that it is impossible for human beings (including criminologists) to be value-neutral or objective in anything, or even to approximate such a state.

Problems also arise when conflict theory is confused with radical theory, as is frequently the case. (Radical theory is presented in the next section.) The two theories are not the same.[60] For example, conflict theory is less specific than radical theory in the identification of causes of crime. Whereas conflict theory specifies stratification or relative powerlessness as criminogenic factors, radical theory focuses on the political and economic structures of society.[61] In this regard, a problem with conflict theory is that it generally fails to identify the sources of power in society.[62] When those sources are identified, power is usually attributed to the personal characteristics of elites (for example, they are smarter, better educated, luckier, and better able to defer immediate gratification). The problem is that conflict theory ignores the social structural sources of power in society (for example, ownership of private property). Conflict theory presumes, in contrast to radical theory, that power is the basis of private property rather than vice versa.[63]

Another major difference between conflict and radical theories is the erroneous assumption, held by conflict theorists, that radical theorists believe that power in society is the exclusive possession of a "capitalist ruling class." Conflict theorists argue, instead, that different groups in society possess and exercise varying degrees of power.[64] In addition, conflict theorists maintain that conflict is not historically or socially limited to a particular type of society (for instance, capitalism), as they assume radical theorists believe. Conflict theorists maintain that conflict is a fundamental element of all societies.[65] The problem is that conflict theorists fundamentally misunderstand the radical position. First, radical theorists do not deny that conflict is a fundamental element of all societies. Second, radical theorists recognize the existence of many conflicting interest groups that wield varying degrees of power in society. However, for radical theorists, the existence of more or less powerful and oftentimes conflicting interest groups does not preclude the existence of "classes" (especially under capitalism); instead, they are considered two different phenomena. The primary difference between interest groups and classes is that usually an individual may voluntarily align him- or herself with any number of interest groups, whereas his or her class position in society is dictated by his or her relation to the means of production, whether or not he or she owns property, and the type of property he or she owns (see next section on radical theory).[66]

A final difference between conflict and radical theories, and a criticism of conflict theory, is that conflict theory is basically reformist—that is, it is not radical.[67] Politically, conflict theory is liberal. Conflict theory assumes that social problems like crime can be corrected by the existing social institutions. Thus, for example, if only the agencies of criminal justice were more effective, a conflict theorist might argue, crime would be greatly reduced. However, historical evidence suggests that this may be a dubious assumption.

RADICAL THEORY

Although the German social theorist Karl Marx (1818–1883) wrote very little about crime and criminal justice, radical theories of crime causation generally are based on a Marxist theoretical framework that interrelates the capitalist mode of production, the state, law, crime control, and crime—as well as other relevant factors.[68] Within this view, there are three competing interpretations of how the aforementioned factors are interrelated: the ruling-class determinist (or instrumentalist), the economic determinist (or structuralist), and the dialectical.

Before examining the three different interpretations, however, some definitions and a brief introduction to Marxist theory might prove useful. First, in Marx's methodology for analyzing society, *historical-materialism*, stages of social history are distinguished by different modes of production. A *mode of production* refers to the means (for example, slavery, feudalism, capitalism, and socialism) by which people produce the material goods necessary for their existence. An individual's relationship to the *means of production* determines his or her *class* position in society (for instance, ruling class or working class) and, ultimately, his or her share of social wealth.[69] In capitalist societies, a numerically small *capitalist ruling class* owns the means of production and receives a greatly disproportionate share of social wealth, primarily by means of rent, interest, and profit. A numerically large *working class*, on the other hand, labors for capitalists to earn wages and receives only a small fraction of social wealth.

Returning to the three interpretations, in the *ruling-class determinist* or *instrumentalist interpretation*, a mostly homogeneous group of capitalists is able to manipulate the state and the law for its own parochial interests. It is able to do this through, among other things, financially controlling political campaigns, especially at the national level. In the *economic determinist* or *structuralist interpretation*, by contrast, the functions of the state are presumed to be determined by structures of society (for example, "the market" or "the law") rather than by people who occupy positions of state power or by individual capitalists. In this version, the survival of the capitalist system, even at the expense of individual capitalists or their agents, is of paramount importance. Finally, the *dialectical interpretation* combines the other two interpretations and adds that which interpretation is more correct at any given time is historically contingent. In the dialectical interpretation, moreover, the state and the law are not viewed only as repressive institutions that promote the interests of the capitalist ruling class over those of all others but also as having liberating potential (for example, antidiscrimination legislation and enforcement). One of the earliest versions of radical theory was introduced by the Dutch socialist, Willem Bonger (1876–1940).[70] Among the first criminologists in the United States to employ one or the other versions of radical theory were Richard Quinney, William J. Chambliss, and Anthony M. Platt (1942–).[71] Also influential in the early development of radical criminology were British criminologists Ian Taylor (1944–), Paul Walton (1944–), and Jock Young (1942–).

In general, radical criminologists focus their attention on the social arrangements of society, especially on political and economic structures and institutions (the "political economy") of *capitalism*. They argue that in capitalist societies, a very small percentage of people are the big winners in the individualistic and competitive struggle for material wealth, and the rest of the population are losers (relatively speaking). The winners (the really big winners are members of the ruling class) do everything in their considerable power (which they possess by virtue of their ownership of material wealth) to keep from becoming losers, including taking advantage of other people—preying on them. Losers (members of the working class and the nonworking classes), in an effort to become winners, usually do what the winners do and prey on weaker people. Radical criminologists believe that the more unevenly wealth is distributed in a society, the more likely people are able to find persons weaker than themselves. Numerous studies support that contention by showing a positive linear relationship between economic inequality and crime rates.[72]

However, it is important to understand that, for radical criminologists, the destructive effects of capitalism, such as crime, are not caused directly by income or property inequality or poverty per se. Rather, crime is a product of the political economy that, in capitalist societies, encourages an individualistic competition among wealthy people and among poor people and between rich and poor people (the intra- and inter*class struggle*) and the practice of taking advantage of other people (*exploitation*). The class struggle and exploitation, in turn, produce crime, income or property inequality, poverty, and many of the other problems that are characteristic of a capitalist society. In short, for radical criminologists, crime in capitalist societies is often a rational response to the circumstances in which people find themselves in the individualistic and competitive struggle to acquire material wealth. Wilson and Herrnstein, though not radical criminologists themselves, suggest that one of the reasons that Japan has much less crime per capita than the United States, even though Japan too is a capitalist society, is the Japanese emphasis on group achievement, as opposed to the American emphasis on individual achievement.[73] The Japanese emphasis on group achievement is derived from the Confucian principle that "the individual is expected to subordinate his own identity to the interest of the group."[74]

According to radical criminologists, "senseless" violent crime, which most often is committed by poor people against each other, frequently is a product of the demoralizing and brutalizing conditions under which many people are forced to live. In short, as Taylor, Walton, and Young explain, "It is not that man behaves [under capitalism] as an animal because of his 'nature': it is that he is not fundamentally allowed by virtue of the social arrangements of production to do otherwise."[75] Elliott Curie (1942–) has recently specified seven elements of "market societies" that, in combination, are likely to breed serious violent crime. They are: (1) "the progressive destruction of livelihood" (the absence of steady well-paying work); (2) "the growth of extremes of economic inequality and material deprivation"; (3) "the withdrawal of public services and supports, especially for families and children"; (4) "the erosion of informal and communal networks of mutual support, supervision, and care"; (5) "the spread of a materialistic, neglectful, and 'hard' culture" (the exaltation of "often brutal individual competition and consumption over the values of community, contribution, and productive work"); (6) "the unregulated marketing of the technology of violence" (the absence of public regulation of firearms); and, not least, (7) "the weakening of social and political alternatives" (which inhibits people most "at risk" from defining their problems in collective terms and envisioning a collective response).[76]

None of this means that noncapitalist societies will be crime-free. Rather noncapitalist societies should have different types of crime and much lower rates of crime (as traditionally defined) "because the less intense class struggle should reduce the forces leading to and the functions of crime."[77]

It is important to emphasize that radical criminologists define the concept of crime differently than is the custom of traditional criminologists. Because they assume that criminal law is all too often manipulated to benefit particular interests to the detriment of all others, radical criminologists argue that the legal definition of crime is both too narrow and too broad in scope. Radical criminologists maintain that "crime" should be defined as a violation of human rights. As Platt explains:

A radical perspective defines crime as a violation of politically-defined human rights: the truly egalitarian rights to decent food and shelter, to human dignity and self-determination, rather than the so-called right to compete for an unequal share of wealth and power.[78]

A radical definition of crime includes "imperialism, racism, capitalism, sexism and other systems of exploitation which contribute to human misery and deprive people of their human potentiality."[79] Although many behaviors currently proscribed by criminal law would be included in this radical definition, other behaviors now considered crimes would be excluded (such as victimless crimes or crimes of consumption), and some behaviors not now considered crimes would be added (such as racism, sexism, imperialism).[80]

Among the policy implications of radical theory is to reconceptualize the definition of crime in terms of violations of human rights. Another is to demonstrate that the criminal law on which the definition of crime currently is based is "used by the state and the ruling class to secure the survival of the capitalist system, and, as capitalist society is further threatened by its own contradictions, criminal law will be increasingly used in the attempt to maintain domestic order."[81] Radical criminologists, following the lead of Marx and Friedrich Engels

(1820–1895), point out that criminal law serves the interests of the ruling class in at least three ways.[82] First, it promotes and protects all private property, even though only a small percentage of the population, which includes the ruling class, owns most of the private property. Second, through concepts such as "justice," "the rule of law," and "equality before the law," criminal law gives the impression that it stands above society as an impartial arbiter of conflicts, thus hiding its origins in political and economic interests, especially those of the ruling class. As Beirne and Messerschmidt observe, "To apply law fairly and equally in a society of inequality is merely to perpetuate inequality."[83] Third, the criminal law is a repressive institution, as noted earlier, able to incapacitate (by imprisoning or executing) people who threaten the capitalist system. Still other implications of radical theory are to expose the criminal justice system as a "state-initiated" and "state-supported" effort to rationalize social control and eventually to replace the criminal justice system with "popular" or "socialist justice."[84]

Consequently, contrary to the beliefs of many liberal criminologists, radical criminologists argue that reform of capitalist institutions, especially those of the criminal justice system, cannot legitimately be expected to eradicate the initial causes of crime for two reasons:

> First, capitalism depends quite substantially on the preservation of the conditions of competition and inequality. Those conditions . . . will tend to lead almost inevitably to relatively pervasive criminal behavior; without those conditions, the capitalist system would scarcely work at all. Second, as many have argued, the general presence of racism in this country, though capitalists may not in fact have created it, tends to support and maintain the power of the capitalists as a class by providing cheap labor and dividing the working class[85]

For nearly all radical criminologists (anarchists are exceptions[86]), the solution to the problem of crime is a socialist society in which human diversity presumably would be appreciated as it is not under capitalism.[87] Such a transformation would in turn require the development of a political consciousness among all people who are exploited and alienated by the capitalist system. Perhaps most importantly for radical criminologists, only through *praxis* (human action based on theory) will the new socialist society be achieved. Currie believes that at present, the most promising lever of change, and at the same time the most effective means to significantly reduce serious violent crime, is "full employment at socially meaningful work at good wages, and with reasonable hours."[88] Such a policy would require "substantially expanding employment in the public and nonprofit sectors of the economy, and developing policies for worksharing and reduction of work time."[89]

One objection to radical theory is that the radical definition of crime as the violation of human rights is itself too broad and vague. Although that view may be true, in a different context, legal philosopher Edmund Cahn noted that although it is often difficult to determine what is just, most people can easily identify what is unjust.[90] Perhaps in a like manner, it may be equally difficult to determine what a human right is, but radical criminologists generally assume that most people know when a human right has been violated.

A second problem with radical theory is the failure to adequately address the question of how working and nonworking people become conscious of their class interests.[91] In other words, how do people learn that they are in a class struggle? To date, the ruling class has been able to effectively undermine the ability of workers (and the unemployed) to become conscious of their class interests by, among other tactics: (1) the creation of job hierarchies and structures of privileges and promotions; (2) the dispersion and disintegration of working-class communities through suburbanization, increasing homeownership (at least until recent years), and geographic mobility; and (3) the creation by the media of a fear of crime that undermines the organization and solidarity of the groups most victimized by crime and most in need of organization and solidarity to realize their interests.[92]

A related problem is the question of how people realize their class interests once they become conscious of them—that is, what is the relationship between theory and praxis?[93] Presumably, class interests are realized through a synthesis of communicative interaction (knowledge) and labor (action), so that actions occasion consciousness of knowledge which in turn informs subsequent action, and so forth.[94] A problem with this explanation is that it fails to account for obvious constraints on consciousness (for example, false consciousness), theoretical knowledge, and practical choice. As Marx pointed out, "The ideas of the ruling class are in every epoch the ruling ideas."[95]

Psychologists have criticized class-based (that is, radical and some critical) theories for ignoring individual differences in the understanding of crime.[96] The argument is that political economy, social structure, and culture are considered constants (and not variables) in class-based theories and that they "cannot account for variation in individual conduct within particular social arrangements" (though they do "have important roles to play in establishing the fundamental contingencies that are in effect within each particular social arrangement").[97] In short, for these critics, political economy, social structure, and culture cannot adequately explain individual differences in criminality (for example, why one type of crime rather than another is committed), but they do determine what stimuli are rewarding or aversive within each particular social arrangement.[98] Many sociologists, on the other hand, believe that social structures and cultures are variables and not constants.[99]

Other criticisms of radical theory are that its adherents are pursuing a political agenda and thus are not objective in their work; that its causal model is wrong—that is, that social arrangements do not cause people to commit crime, as radical theorists argue, but rather that crime is committed by people who are born evil and remain evil; that it has not been tested satisfactorily; that it cannot be tested satisfactorily; and that it is utopian in its policy implications.[100]

The accusation of utopianism (*utopia* means "nowhere") is most frequently directed at radical theory's assumption that socialism is the solution to the crime problem in capitalist societies. At a time when many so-called socialist or communist nations are racing to adopt free-market economies (capitalism), the assumption seems questionable at best. However, radical criminologists maintain that none of the nations that have claimed to be socialist or communist were or are truly socialist or communist, at least as Marx had originally conceived the terms. They say it is unfair to look to the totalitarian nations that were socialist or communist in name only for guidance in dealing with the crime problems of capitalist societies.

Today, it probably makes little sense to speak of capitalist and socialist societies anyway, because no pure societies of either type exist. (They probably never did.) All countries now manifest elements of both capitalism and socialism. In the United States, for example, Social Security, Medicare, Medicaid, and other social programs provided by federal, state, and local governments are clearly socialistic, as is so-called corporate welfare, such as the many subsidies and tax loopholes for corporations. Thus, as we begin the twenty-first century, we must recognize that all countries have "mixed" economies, with elements of both capitalism and socialism. A key question, then, especially for those people who are interested in reducing the crime problem and improving the overall quality of human life, is, What is the best mix?

OTHER CRITICAL THEORIES

The politically conservative law-and-order climate of the 1980s and 1990s was not a period in which critical theories of crime causation received much attention from government bureaucrats and criminal justice practitioners. Nevertheless, critical scholars continued to produce and refine critical analyses of government efforts to understand and to address the crime problem. In this section, some of the new directions taken by critical theorists are described to show the diversity of current critical thought.[101]

British or Left Realism

The focus of many critical criminologists has been on crimes committed by the powerful. While pursuing that area of study, however, they have tended either to ignore or to romanticize working-class crime and criminals. By the mid-1980s, a group of social scientists in Great Britain had begun to criticize that tendency and to argue that critical criminologists needed to redirect their attention to the fear and the very real victimization experienced by working-class individuals.[102] These "left realists" correctly observed that crimes against the working class were being perpetrated not only by the powerful but also by members of the working class. They admonished their critical colleagues to take crime seriously, especially street crime and domestic violence. Recently, one of the leading exponents of left realism, Jock Young, has identified relative deprivation as a potent, though not exclusive, cause of crime.[103]

Not willing to wait for the socialist revolution promised by "left idealists" and, by default, cede criminal justice policy to conservative law-and-order types, left realists have argued that, among other things, police power must be employed to protect people living in working-class communities. Also advocated by left realists are greater community involvement and dealing with structural problems that cause offending. Examples of the latter include reducing unfair income inequities and providing good jobs with a future, neighborhoods of which residents can be proud, and community facilities that enhance a sense of cohesion and belonging.[104]

Left realism has been criticized for holding a contradictory position toward the state. On the one hand, left realists want to give the state more power to combat crime, especially crime committed against the working class. On the other hand, they want to reduce the power of the state to intervene in citizens' lives and make the state more accountable for its actions.[105] Another criticism is that in their effort to focus attention on crimes committed against the working class, left realists have deflected attention from white-collar and government crimes.[106] Left realism's emphasis on the reform of criminal justice practice, rather than on radical change, has been criticized for being little different from traditional, mainstream criminology.[107] Finally, feminists have argued that left realists, like most radical and critical criminologists, have remained "gender blind" and "gender biased," failing to appreciate the "activism, research, and theory drawn from women's experiences."[108]

Peacemaking Criminology

This perspective rejects the idea that predatory criminal violence can be reduced by repressive state violence. In this view, "wars" on crime only make matters worse. Consisting of a mixture of anarchism, humanism, socialism, and Native American and Eastern philosophies, peacemaking criminology suggests that the solution to all social problems, including crime, is the transformation of human beings, mutual dependence, reduction of hierarchical structures, the creation of communities of caring people, and universal social justice. For peacemaking criminologists, such as Hal Pepinsky (1945–) and Richard Quinney,[109] crime is suffering, and, therefore, to reduce crime, suffering must be reduced. Emphasis is placed on the transformation of human beings, on an inner rebirth or spiritual rejuvenation (inner peace) that enables individuals to experience empathy with those less fortunate and respond to other people's needs. Peacemaking criminologists also advocate "restorative justice," which was discussed previously as a policy implication of interactionism and labeling theories. In short, for peacemaking criminologists, it is necessary for people to first change themselves before they can change the world.

Peacemaking criminology can be criticized for its extreme idealism and emphasis on the transformation of individuals (as a way of transforming society) rather than the transformation of society (as a way of transforming individuals). It has also been criticized for not providing a blueprint of how such transformations can be achieved.[110]

Feminism

Although feminism is not new, its application to the study of crime is.[111] Recognizing that the study of crime always has been androcentric, feminist criminologists seek a feminine perspective. Specifically, the focus of feminist analyses is on women's experiences and ways of knowing because, in the past, men's experiences have been taken as the norm and generalized to the population. As a result, women and girls have been omitted almost entirely from general theories of crime and delinquency.

Three areas of crime and justice have commanded most of feminist theorists' attention: (1) the victimization of women, (2) gender differences in crime, and (3) gendered justice (that is, the treatment of women and girls by the agencies and agents of criminal justice). Regarding gender differences in crime, two questions seem to dominate: Do explanations of male criminality apply to women? Why are women less likely than men to engage in crime?

Not all feminists share the same perspective on the issues noted. At least four different types of feminist thought have been identified: liberal, radical, Marxist, and socialist. (Conspicuously omitted from this typology are women of color, whose gender and race place them in a uniquely disadvantaged position).[112] The latter three types of feminist thought, to varying degrees, share a belief that the problems of women, including female victimization, lie in the institution of *patriarchy* (men's control over women's labor and sexuality).

Liberal feminists are the exception. They do not generally view discrimination against women as systemic or the product of patriarchy. For them, the solution to women's subordinate position in society is the removal of obstacles to their full participation in social life. Liberal feminists seek equal opportunity, equal rights, and freedom of choice. As for crime, liberal feminists point to gender socialization (that is, the creation of masculine and feminine identities) as the primary culprit.[113]

Marxist feminists, as noted, view patriarchal oppression as the fundamental problem for women. For them, the solution lies in the transformation of capitalism to socialism. They envision a socialist society where housework and child care are socialized, marriage and other sexual relations based on ideas of private property are abolished, and working-class economic subordination is eliminated.[114]

Radical feminists argue that patriarchal relations predate both class and private property as sources of women's oppression. Consequently, a socialist society that has not eliminated patriarchal relations will do little to emancipate women from their subordinate position. For radical feminists, the goal is the abolition of patriarchal relationships.[115]

Finally, socialist feminists combine the positions of radical and Marxist feminists by viewing gender and class relations as coequal sources of oppression. They seek to transform patriarchal and capitalist class relations simultaneously.[116]

One of the principal criticisms of feminist criminology, as noted previously, is the focus on gender as a central organizing theme. Such a focus fails to appreciate differences among women—for example, differences between the experiences of black and white women.[117] It also elevates gender to the critical factor in explaining crime, even though it is not the most critical factor always or in all situations. In some cases, race or class, for example, may be equally or more important.[118] Another problem, similar to the one associated with left realism, is many feminists' contradictory position toward the state. On the one hand, several feminists call for greater use of the state and its agents to better protect women from abuse; on the other hand, some feminists concede that giving more power to the state and its agents, under present circumstances, will only lead to further discrimination and harassment of minority males and females.[119] A similar contradictory position is held by many feminists toward using the law to improve gender relations. The law, after all, is almost entirely the product of white males.

Postmodernism and Poststructuralism

Postmodernism and *poststructuralism* are directions in critical theory that are difficult to both define and comprehend. They originated in the late 1960s as a rejection of the "modern" or Enlightenment belief in scientific rationality as the route to knowledge and progress. Emphasized, instead, is the importance of the unconscious (as conceptualized by Freud), free-floating signs and images, and a plurality of viewpoints. Postmodernist ideas began to be introduced in law and criminology during the late 1980s.[120]

Subfields of postmodernism and poststructuralism are *semiotics* (the science of how signs produce meaning) and *deconstruction* (the rhetorical interpretation of texts or society to reverse any structural hierarchy that might be present). The goals of this area of critical thought are to understand the creation of knowledge, and how knowledge and language create hierarchy and domination. As applied to the area of crime and criminal justice, the major foci have been critical analyses of the privileged position of "the Law" and the construction of crime theories.[121]

With regard to "the Law," postmodernist criminologists reject the idea "that there is only one true interpretation of a law or for that matter the U.S. Constitution."[122] They argue, instead, that there is a plurality of interpretations that are dependent, in part, on the particular social context in which they arise. Like in other critical criminologies, the law, from a postmodernist view, always has a human author and a political agenda.[123] As for crime theories, postmodernist criminologists typically abandon the usual notion of causation. From the postmodernist perspective:

> crime is seen to be the culmination of certain processes that allow persons to believe that they are somehow not connected to other humans and society. These processes place others into categories or stereotypes and make them different or alien, denying them their humanity. These processes result in the denial of responsibility for other people and to other people.[124]

Postmodernist criminologists would replace the formal criminal justice apparatus with informal social controls so that the current functions of criminal justice are handled by local groups and local communities.[125] This strategy is consistent with the one advocated by peacemaking criminologists.

Postmodernism and deconstructionist analysis, especially the more radical versions, have been criticized "for not valuing anything, and for a belief that 'anything goes' . . . for being an anarchy of knowledge . . . [for their] subjectivism, plural relativism, and nihilism."[126] In short, as Einstadter and Henry ask, "If truth is not possible, how can we decide anything?"[127] Some critical criminologists, most notably Stuart Henry (1949–) and Dragan Milovanovic (1948–), have attempted to overcome those charges and have used postmodernist thought to create a "constitutive criminology."[128]

Henry and Milovanovic's *constitutive criminology*, unlike skeptical versions of postmodernism, which they characterize as nihilistic, subjective, and defeatist, offers an affirmative, optimistic, and humanistic approach emphasizing reconstruction and redirection. Ultimately, Henry and Milovanovic hope their theory will inform social policies that produce less, rather than more harm.

Constitutive criminology assumes that human beings socially construct their world primarily through language and symbolic representation but, at the same time, are also shaped by the world they create. Two contradictions of this process are that (1) people come to reify the world they create (that is, they forget, if they ever knew, that they are producers of their social world) and (2) the institutions and structures people create frequently become the sources of social constraint and domination—as do attempts to oppose them. The optimism of Henry and Milovanovic's theory lies in the belief that, as creators, human beings are capable of changing the institutions and structures that dominate and constrain them. In constitutive criminology, people are "coproducers" of reality and their actions can be both constraining and liberating.

Thus, humans are also coproducers of crime—"the ultimate form of reification"—because of the social and organizational structures they create. Crime, in this theory, is a "socially constructed and discursively constituted category." It is "the power to deny others," "to create harm (pain) in any context," or to render "others powerless to make their own difference." Criminals are "'excessive investors' in the accumulation and expression of power and control." They are not, however, a distinct category in constitutive criminology as they are in most modernist theories. In constitutive criminology, there is continuity and interrelatedness between law-abiding and law-violating or between harm-reducing and harm-producing (see Matza's theory of drift).[129]

In short, constitutive criminology presumes that crime is the result of powerlessness or power differentials—the position of liberal as opposed to more radical versions of conflict theory. It also incorporates a tenet of early labeling theory that "crime feeds off itself, expanding and consuming the energies intended to control it." A problem with this conceptualization is that, like liberal versions of conflict theory, sources of power and power differentials in constitutive criminology are not fully explained or appreciated. By focusing on the linguistic production of reality, Henry and Milovanovic tend to downplay (but do not ignore) the relationship between power and the material conditions of production, such as the ownership of private property and wealth.

The general policy implications of constitutive criminology are twofold: (1) "crime must be deconstructed as a recurrent discursive [that is, linguistic] process," and (2) "conscious attempts must be made at reconstruction with a view to preventing [crime's] recurrence." The primary way to accomplish those policies is "the development of alternative, 'replacement discourses' that fuel positive social constructions . . . designed to displace crime as moments in the exercise of power as control." "Discourses" are the prevailing ways of describing the world. Replacement discourses, created by "cultural revolutionaries," will deconstruct prevailing meanings and displace them with "new conceptions, distinctions, words and phrases, which convey alternative meanings."[130] A classic example of replacement discourse is Sutherland's concept of "white-collar crime," which he successfully introduced into the criminological lexicon. Replacement discourses will "tell different stories" about the world as experienced by historically subjugated people. Through their discursive diversity, replacement discourses celebrate "unofficial, informal, discounted and ignored knowledges." The creation of replacement discourses is an ongoing struggle.

Henry and Milovanovic stress that replacement discourses, once created, must extend beyond the walls of academia to the public arena through such avenues as the news media and popular culture. The primary vehicle for accomplishing this goal is Barak's "newsmaking criminology," where criminologists proactively demystify or deconstruct crime stories presented by the media and offer more authentic crime stories of their own.[131]

In conjunction with replacement discourses, a second harm-reduction strategy is "radical refraction" or "social judo," through which excessive investors in "the reality of power are turned away from harm production, and toward reinvesting in positive connections with a relationally oriented community of fellow human subjects." The judo metaphor is apt here because, on the one hand, Henry and Milovanovic argue that using power to reduce the power of others only replaces one excessive investor with another. On the other hand, when using judo as a means of self-defense, the power of the aggressor is turned back against the aggressor to bring about his or her ultimate defeat. Other ways of reorienting excessive investors include promoting shared responsibility and cooperation by increasing face-to-face interactions among people, "peacemaking conflict reduction," and therapeutic "narrative revisions."[132]

A third harm-reduction strategy is to help "constituted victims" become recovering subjects within their local communities. This could be accomplished through the use of support or self-help groups that would empower victims who share similar experiences and situations.

Most importantly, if any of the aforementioned strategies is to be successful, there must be a transformation or reorganization of the political economy. For Henry and Milovanovic, the best hope for societal-level or structural transformation is a variant of Roberto Unger's (1947–) "superliberalism" (that is, a practical, political philosophy that aims to maximize diversity and minimize hegemony by creating "a society in which people are more fully empowered through the development of institutional arrangements that both diminish the gap between framework-preserving routine and framework-transforming conflict and weaken the established forms of social division and hierarchy").[133] Henry and Milovanovic expect that such structural transformation, as well as the other strategies described earlier, will meet with resistance as excessive investors use all means at their disposal (such as cooptation and subversion) to undermine it. Consequently, the societal and cultural transformations advocated in constitutive criminology will require continuous and relentless social struggle.

STUDY QUESTIONS

Critical Theories

1. What are the origins of critical theory in the United States?
2. How do critical theories differ from classical/neoclassical and positivist theories?

Interactionism and Labeling Theory

3. What contribution to crime causation theory does interactionism make?
4. How would interactionist and labeling theorists explain crime?
5. How would they prevent crime?

6. What are problems with interactionist and labeling theories?

7. How do interactionist and labeling theories compare with theories described in previous chapters?

Conflict Theory

8. How do conflict theorists explain crime?

9. How would conflict theorists prevent crime?

10. What are problems with conflict theories of crime causation?

11. How does conflict theory compare with theories described previously in this book?

Radical Theory

12. What are the three models of society for radical theorists?

13. How do radical theorists explain crime?

14. How would radical theorists prevent crime?

15. What are problems with radical theories of crime causation?

16. How does radical theory compare with theories described previously in this book?

Other Critical Theories

17. What are some of the newer critical theory perspectives?

18. What are some of the policy implications of the newer critical theory perspectives?

19. What are problems with the newer critical theory perspectives?

20. How do the newer critical theory perspectives compare with theories described previously in this book?

NOTES

1. See Mills (1970, originally published in 1956); also see Gouldner (1971); Zinn (1990); Simon (1996).

2. See Chomsky (1969); also see Gouldner (1971).

3. Lanier and Henry (1998:236).

4. See Taylor et al. (1974:213).

5. See Bohm (1981); Howe (1997).

6. See Gouldner (1971:Chap. 13).

7. Vold and Bernard (1986:250).

8. See Vold (1979:253).

9. See Vold (1979:254).

10. Vold (1979:254).

11. Blumer (1969:2).

12. See Vold (1979:255–256).

13. See Dowie (1977).

14. Blumer (1969:2).

15. See Vold (1979:256).

16. Blumer (1969:2).

17. See Vold (1979:256).

18. See Vold (1979:256).

19. Vold (1979:258).

20. Vold and Bernard (1986:253–254).

21. See Vold (1979:256–257).

22. Vold (1979:257); Taylor et al. (1974:142).

23. Cooley (1964); also see Vold (1979:257).

24. Becker (1963:9). Lanier and Henry (1998:167) observe that whereas social control theories view clear moral labeling of behavior as important, labeling theory views such labeling as the problem.

25. Lemert (1951).

26. Martin et al. (1990:216).

27. Schur (1973).

28. Lilly et al. (1989:131–135).

29. Vold and Bernard (1986:255); National Institute (1977:136); Taylor et al. (1974:140–141).

30. Braithwaite (1989).

31. Another form of restorative justice is "participatory justice," see Stephens (1987).

32. Braithwaite (1989:61–65).

33. See Davis (1975:165).

34. Becker (1963).

35. Martin et al. (1990:371).

36. Martin et al. (1990:372).

37. See Taylor et al. (1974:153–155).

38. Vold and Bernard (1986:256); also see Akers (1967).

39. Vold and Bernard (1986:256).

40. Vold and Bernard (1986:256).

41. Vold and Bernard (1986:256).

42. Vold and Bernard (1986:256).

43. Martin et al. (1990:369).

44. Andrews and Bonta (1994:197); Hudson (1997).

45. See Davis (1975:179).

46. Becker (1963:9).

47. See Vold (1979:266).

48. Vold (1958); Sellin (1938); Turk (1969); Quinney (1970); Chambliss and Seidman (1971). Sellin's is a theory of culture conflict and not the conflict of competing interest groups. Sellin has been criticized for overemphasizing the extent of culture conflict in society (see Kornhauser, 1978:182–186). Quinney and Chambliss were considered conflict theorists before they became identified with radical theory. Quinney has since moved on to peacemaking criminology (which is presented in a later section of this chapter).

49. See Davis (1975:193).

50. See Vold and Bernard (1986:293).

51. Vold and Bernard (1986:294).

52. Vold and Bernard (1986:294).

53. See Vold and Bernard (1986:295–296).

54. Andrews and Bonta (1994:95–96).

55. Tittle (1995:7).

56. See Dahrendorf (1959:171); Messerschmidt (1997:71).

57. Skogan (1990:5).

58. Bohm (1981).

59. Turk (1979:464).

60. The two theories are sometimes distinguished as "pluralistic-conflict theory" and "class-conflict theory." The former refers to the conflict theory presented in this section; the latter refers to the radical theory presented in the next section.

61. See Bohm (1982).

62. See Bohm (1982).

63. See Bohm (1982).

64. See Bohm (1982).

65. See Bohm (1982).

66. See Bohm (1982).

67. See Bohm (1982).

68. Much of the following discussion is from Bohm (1982); also see Lynch and Groves (1989).

69. Beirne and Messerschmidt (2000:102) maintain that "class position is an important determinant of such basic life events as social mobility, consciousness, level and types of education and income, leisure patterns, and . . . the likelihood of incarceration."

70. See Bonger (1916).

71. See note 48.

72. See Vold and Bernard (1986:141).

73. Wilson and Herrnstein (1985:455–456).

74. Wilson and Herrnstein (1985:455–456).

75. Taylor et al. (1975:23).

76. Currie (1997a); also see Currie (1997b).

77. Chambliss (1976:9).

78. Platt (1975:103).

79. Platt (1975:103); also see Schwendinger and Schwendinger (1975) for a similar definition.

80. Although racism and sexism are not explicitly illegal, hate-crime legislation has been enacted that enhances the penalties for crimes that are motivated by an offender's bias against a race, a religion, an ethnic/national origin group, or a sexual-orientation group. See Jacobs (1998).

81. Quinney (1974:16). Among the contradictions of capitalism are structured unemployment (where a 4 or 5 percent peacetime unemployment rate is generally considered "full employment"); the exportation of higher-paying manufacturing jobs to Third World countries and their replacement with lower-paying service-sector jobs (the service-sector jobs also frequently lack the health and retirement benefits commonly available with manufacturing jobs); inflation (which occurs when the supply of goods fails to meet the demand); recession (which is a temporary decline in business activity during a period when such activity has been generally increasing); and depression (which is a period marked by a decrease of business activity, greatly increased unemployment, falling prices and wages, and so forth).

82. See Beirne and Messerschmidt (2000:105).

83. Beirne and Messerschmidt (2000:105).

84. Quinney (1977:10, 22–23).

85. D. Gordon (1976:206).

86. For a description of "anarchist criminology," see Ferrell (1997, 1999).

87. Taylor et al. (1974:282).

88. Currie (1997a:168).

89. Currie (1997a:168).

90. Cahn (1966).

91. Bohm (1981).

92. Regarding the first two tactics, see Wright (1978:100–101). Regarding the third tactic, in a recent longitudinal analysis, Beckett (1997) shows that political rhetoric about

crime precedes increases in citizen concerns about crime. She suggests that political elites manipulate public perceptions of crime and what should be done about it ("getting tough") ostensibly for political gain.

93. See Bohm (1981).

94. See Gouldner (1976).

95. Marx and Engels (1970:64).

96. Andrews and Bonta (1994:95–96); also see Tittle (1995:7).

97. Andrews and Bonta (1994:113–114).

98. See criticisms of learning theories.

99. See, for example, Kornhauser (1978:Chap. 1).

100. See Lynch and Groves (1989) for a discussion of those criticisms; also see Einstadter and Henry (1995:253–257).

101. Much of the following discussion is from Schwartz (1989) and MacLean and Milovanovic (1997).

102. See, for example, Lea and Young (1984); Kinsey et al. (1986); Matthews and Young (1986); also see Schwartz and DeKeseredy (1991) for a review and critique of this position.

103. Young (1997:30).

104. Young (1997:30 and 35).

105. Einstadter and Henry (1995:256).

106. Einstadter and Henry (1995:256); Michalowski (1990).

107. Einstadter and Henry (1995:257); Michalowski (1990).

108. Cited in Einstadter and Henry (1995:257).

109. See Pepinsky and Quinney (1991); Pepinsky (1999); Pepinsky and Quinney (1997); Sullivan (1980).

110. Beirne and Messerschmidt (2000:237).

111. For excellent reviews and examples, see Daly and Chesney-Lind (1988); Simpson (1989); Daly and Maher (1998); Chesney-Lind and Bloom (1997); also see Williams and McShane (1994:230–240) and Beirne and Messerschmidt (2000:202–209).

112. Also omitted from the typology are other possible subdivisions, see Einstadter and Henry (1995:263–264).

113. For an example of liberal feminist theory, see Simon (1975).

114. For examples of Marxist feminist theory, see Balkan et al. (1980) and Schwendinger and Schwendinger (1983).

115. For an example of radical feminist theory, see Stanko (1985).

116. For examples of socialist feminist theory, see Messerschmidt (1986); Jurik (1999).

117. Einstadter and Henry (1995:275).

118. Messerschmidt (1997:70–71).

119. Einstadter and Henry (1995:275).

120. Einstadter and Henry (1995:278).

121. See, for example, Ferrell (1993); Henry and Milovanovic (1991); Pfohl and Gordon (1986).

122. Cited in Einstadter and Henry (1995:287).

123. Arrigo and Young (1997:77).

124. Einstadter and Henry (1995:291).

125. Einstadter and Henry (1995:294).

126. Einstadter and Henry (1995:280).

127. Einstadter and Henry (1995:280).

128. Henry and Milovanovic (1991); Henry and Milovanovic (1996); also see Barak et al. (1997).

129. Matza (1964).

130. Also see Arrigo and Young (1997:81–82).

131. Barak (1988, 1994).

132. See Arrigo and Young (1997:82–83) for a description of "transpraxis," the concept they use for the vehicle by which society can be transformed into a more "humanistic and just social order."

133. Unger (1987).

8

⊞

Conclusion: Integrated Theories And Beyond

B ecause theories of crime and delinquency have been produced by scholars representing several different academic disciplines, the review of theories in this book is reminiscent of the story about the blind people and the elephant. The story goes something like this: Several blind people encountered an elephant. Attempting to describe it, each of the blind people felt a different part. One person felt the elephant's tail and described the elephant as long and hairy. Another felt the elephant's ear and described the elephant as rough and leathery. Still another blind person felt the elephant's tusk and described the elephant as smooth and long. Get the idea? Each of the blind people felt only a part of the elephant and believed that what they felt described the elephant as a whole. However, none of the blind people actually described the elephant accurately. In an analogous way, scholars trying to understand criminality and delinquency generally have examined only a part of the phenomenon and only from the vantage of their particular discipline. None of them probably has explained the phenomenon completely, which would be an imposing task even if they could agree on what the phenomenon they are trying to explain really is.

The multidisciplinary nature of crime theory production is both a benefit and a curse. The benefit stems from the many different perspectives and bodies of knowledge that are applied to the subject matter. The causes of crime probably have been analyzed with a greater disciplinary breadth than most other academic subject matters. The curse, as already noted, is that analyses of the causes of crime generally have not been interdisciplinary. The questions that have been asked and the answers that have been given, for the most part, have remained within the province of a particular academic discipline. The result has been biological reductionism, psychological reductionism, sociological reductionism, and so forth. In this context, *reductionism* is the discipline-specific use of concepts that are considered to cause criminal or delinquent behavior.[1]

Tittle calls the resulting theories "simple theories," which he characterizes as consisting of "one or two explanatory principles involving only a few variables that are assumed to apply to all instances of the particular form of deviance [crime] being explained."[2] Most of the theories of crime and delinquency presented in the previous chapters are simple theories, according to Tittle. The problem with simple theories, observes Tittle, is that they may seem reasonable, have some (but never compelling) empirical support, and have attracted followers, but none of them has much explanatory power (see the discussion in Chapter 1). Thus, to increase explanatory power, overcome charges of reductionism, and for other reasons (such as reducing the number of competing theories), "integrated" theories of crime causation have been created.[3]

What Tittle calls simple theories are, for the most part, really simple integrated theories because, as he defines them, they are typically comprised of at least two explanatory principles and a few variables. As noted in Chapter 3, early positivists long ago advocated and employed multifactor approaches; some even recognized the need for theorists to integrate biological, psychological, and sociological influences. Many recent positivists and some critical theorists have followed this trend. What distinguishes simple integrated theories from more elaborate integrated theories are the number of concepts (and variables) employed, the degree of specification of how those concepts are combined or interact, and, oftentimes, the range of crime types to be explained.

For discussion purposes, it may prove useful to consider four different types of integrated theory. First are theories that integrate or synthesize concepts from different theories within the same discipline, for example, some combination of concepts from the following sociological theories: social disorganization theory, anomie or strain theory, learning theories, and social control theories. An example of this type of theory is Delbert Elliot (1933–) and his colleagues' theory of delinquency and illegal drug use. They contend that social disorganization, strain, and inadequate socialization combine to weaken conventional bonding and strengthen delinquent bonding. This, in turn, causes delinquent behavior, including illegal drug use. Concepts from social learning theory are used to explain the weakening and strengthening of bonds. The social control components of the theory are emphasized over the social learning components.[4]

Second are theories that combine theories or concepts from different disciplines within the same paradigm, for instance, the integration of theories or concepts from biological positivism, psychological positivism, and sociological positivism. This type of integration usually requires the synthesis of theories or concepts at different levels of analysis, for example, the integration of concepts from biological and psychological theories (individual level of analysis) with concepts from sociological theories (aggregate, group, or societal level of analysis). Many of the theories described in Chapters 4, 5, and 6 are examples of this type of integrated theory.[5] Another example is Henry and Milovanovic's critical, postmodern constitutive theory, described in Chapter 7.[6]

Third are theories, referred to as developmental or life-course theories, that posit that different factors (sometimes from different disciplines and different levels of analysis) affect people's propensity for crime at different times in their lives. So, for example, during childhood, the family may be the most important influence in determining whether a child engages in delinquency; during adolescence, peer group influences may be most important; and during adulthood, marital and occupational relations may predominate. Any factor that is influential at one point in a person's life may be irrelevant at another time. An example of this type of theory is Robert Sampson (1956–) and John Laub's (1953–) theory of social bonding across the life course.[7] Like Hirschi and other social control theorists, Sampson and Laub argue that crime and delinquency are likely to occur when an individual's bond to society is weakened or broken. What is unique about their theory is that the important elements of the social bond change over the life course. Specifically, Sampson and Laub contend that a wide variety of individual and social structural factors (such as socioeconomic disadvantage, broken homes, family disruption, parental criminality, household crowding, large family size, residential mobility, and mother's employment) affect both informal social controls and social capital, which, in turn, affect crime and delinquency. Social capital refers to social relationships (for example, parent-child, teacher-student, or employer-employee) that can become social and psychological resources that can reduce the chances of criminal or delinquent behavior. Thus, for Sampson and Laub, adolescent delinquency is often the product of individual and social structural factors mediated by little social capital and weakened social controls (inadequate family socialization and school attachment and the influence of

delinquent siblings and peers). Adult deviance and criminality are sometimes, but not always, a function of antisocial and delinquent behavior in
childhood. The critical factors in adult crime and deviance are again the
social bond and social capital. Strong social bonds (for example, strong
social ties to jobs and family) and social capital reduce the likelihood of
crime and deviance; conversely, weak social bonds and little social capital increase the likelihood of crime and deviance. Developmental or life-
course theorists frequently refer to people who persistently commit
crime over their life course as "career criminals." Only a very small percentage of all offenders are believed to be career criminals. For most
offenders, criminal behavior can begin or end anytime during their lives,
though, for most offenders, it is likely to end by the time they reach their
late 30s or early 40s.

Fourth are theories that attempt to integrate theories or concepts
from different paradigms or to combine all of the different types of integration, for example, theories that attempt to synthesize classical, positivist, or critical theories or concepts.[8] Some of these theories are quite
elaborate. For example, Bryan Vila (1947–) has created a holistic theory comprised of ecological, micro-level, and macro-level factors
which, he argues, interact and influence a wide range of criminal
behaviors depending on individual developmental factors over the life
course and across generations.[9] He also maintains that a statistical model
based on mathematical nonlinear chaos theory rather than on more traditional statistical analytic models may be a more useful and accurate
way to test his integrated theory. Taking a different tack, Gregg Barak
(1948–) has recently proposed a "post-postmodern synthesis."[10] Barak
advocates the combining, in a truly interdisciplinary approach, the different types of knowledges that have something to say about crime and
criminality. He lists knowledges from "economics, philosophy, anthropology, biochemistry, psychology, law, sociology, cultural studies, ethnic
studies, gender studies, media studies, political economy, and social history" as prime candidates for this type of integration.[11] At the same
time, Barak also doubts whether different theories and concepts can
ever be successfully integrated,[12] so it remains to be seen what is to be
integrated from the different knowledges if not theories and concepts.

To date, none of the efforts at theory integration has proven especially compelling.[13] Though not a criticism per se, it is interesting to
observe that in none of the integrations are the different theories or
concepts given equal weight. One of the theories or concepts or a
group of theories always predominates. Consequently, the integrations
often turn out to be, for example, control theories with learning theory or anomie or strain theory additions or psychological theories with
biological and sociological considerations.

At the extreme, theory integration is sometimes little more than an exercise in throwing into a statistical model everything including the kitchen sink to explain more of the variation in the dependent variable crime.[14] Although combining factors such as gender, race, age, place of residence, IQ, aggressiveness, level of self-control, conditions of childhood training, prior offenses, peer relationships, and social bonds, allows a researcher to predict criminal behavior with a fair degree of accuracy, it does not begin to answer the questions of why or how those factors are related either to each other or, more importantly, to criminal behavior.[15] It is also impossible to determine whether or not the relationships in such models are spurious. Such statistical modeling, then, is really not theory integration at all.

Testing integrated theories may be another problem, especially if the theories or concepts to be combined are at different levels of analysis. Theories or concepts at the individual level of analysis should only be tested with individual-level data, whereas theories or concepts at the aggregate, group, or societal level of analysis should only be tested with aggregate-level data. Attempting to test theories or concepts with data at an inappropriate level of analysis results in the ecological fallacy described in Chapter 1.[16] New methods of statistical analysis, however, may be able to overcome this problem.[17]

Two other methodological problems with some attempts at theory integration are (1) the failure to specify the sequencing or the temporal ordering of factors, and (2) the failure to consider reciprocal effects or interactions among concepts.[18] So, for example, does a bad family life determine whether a child drops out of school and, as a result, engages in delinquency? Or does delinquency cause a child to drop out of school and, consequently, have a bad family life? Or does dropping out of school reduce the quality of family life, which causes delinquency? And so forth. Research suggests that in all cases the relationships are probably reciprocal or interactive. In other words, dropping out of school, a bad family life, and delinquency may each be cause and effect of the other (but not necessarily for all people and at all times during the life course). In short, there may not be any correct ordering of factors. Thus, in this example, it is probably inaccurate to argue that either dropping out of school or a bad family life necessarily precedes delinquency in time.[19]

Some critics contend that the combining of certain concepts or assumptions produces logical inconsistencies. They ask, for example, how is it possible "that crime is caused by successful and unsuccessful socialization, control and lack of control, individualistic and group goals, social and nonsocial reinforcement, and contact with deviant and conventional others"?[20] They also wonder how criminal behavior can be both freewilled and determined at the same time, or how both consensus and conflict over moral values can simultaneously characterize society.[21] For that matter and more broadly, they wonder whether crime is the response of an abnormal individual to a normal environment, or whether crime is the response of a normal individual to an abnormal environment. How could it be both? Critics, in short, argue that the integration of some theories has been accomplished only by ignoring philosophical assumptions or misrepresenting or distorting the theories or concepts to be combined.

These presumed logical inconsistencies, moreover, are crucial when it comes to policy. For example, if crime is the response of a freewilled or abnormal individual to a normal environment, then it makes sense to focus crime control policy on individuals (for example, deterrence or rehabilitation). On the other hand, if crime is the response of a determined or normal individual to an abnormal environment, then it makes sense to direct crime control policy to changing the environment (for instance, providing opportunity or strengthening communities). It makes little sense to do both.

The charge of logical inconsistency, however, only applies to positivist or classical/neoclassical syntheses, in which the conceptual or philosophical dichotomies or categories are presumed to accurately represent phenomena in the real world. To the critical theorist, conceptual or philosophical dichotomies or categories are at best heuristic devices that necessarily distort reality. They are false dichotomies. For the critical theorist, human beings are neither freewilled nor determined but are both freewilled and determined. In other words, human beings are free to choose within biological, psychological, and sociological constraints. Human beings not only shape the world, but also are shaped by it. Likewise, for critical theorists, society is characterized by neither consensus nor conflict over moral values but is instead a reflection of both consensus and conflict over moral values (though conflict is likely to predominate). Finally, neither individuals nor societies are normal or abnormal. To the extent that the two concepts have any meaning at all, individuals and societies manifest both normal and abnormal qualities along a continuum. In short, for critical theorists, there is always a dialectical relationship between invented categories of individuals or societies.

As for policy implications, if the dialectic more accurately describes the relationships between individuals and the societies in which they live, then the choice of policies may depend primarily on utility. In other words, since policies can be directed toward individuals, social institutions, or both, one of three choices must prevail if anything is going to be done at all. First, policies could be directed toward individuals. Such a choice would require the changing of individuals—in many cases, one person at a time—which seems like an incredibly inefficient way of producing change. Second, policies could be directed toward changing social institutions which seems like a less intrusive and much more efficient strategy for changing large numbers of people. Such a policy, however, would have to be sensitive to individual differences and undoubtedly would allow some individuals to "fall through the cracks." Third, policies could be directed toward changing individuals and social institutions simultaneously. However, this policy seems less efficient than the second one and is likely to squander scarce resources if the ultimate goal is to change the behavior of large numbers of people.

In any event, probably the best way to make sense of the various theories examined in this book is to begin with a consideration of their philosophical assumptions. As mentioned in Chapter 1, whether a theory is accepted or rejected often depends on whether one believes in a theory's philosophical assumptions rather than on the scientific support (or lack of support) for the theory. A principal reason for this state of affairs, as noted in Chapter 1, is that scientific research into the causes of crime almost never offers a critical test that supports one competing theory over another.

As for philosophical assumptions, do you believe that human beings are freewilled and completely responsible for their behavior? Do you believe that they are motivated by pleasure-pain, risk-reward, or cost-benefit rationality? Do you believe that society is based on a social contract? If your answer to those three questions is yes, then you probably find classical theory most compelling. Even if you believe that human beings are not completely freewilled and responsible for their behavior, but you still believe in hedonistic or other calculating kind of rationality as the basis of human motivation and social contract as the basis of society, then you probably find the neoclassical revision most compelling.

On the other hand, if you believe that human beings are determined (either in a "hard" or "soft" way) and that society is based primarily on a consensus (by either the collective conscience or division of labor, but not a social contract), then you probably find one of the positivist theories most compelling. If so, then you can narrow your choice or choices of theories by critically assessing the problems associated with each of the theories. Ask yourself, Are any of the problems critical enough to disqualify the theory? If your answer is yes, then reject the theory.[22] If any theory survives this exercise, then it must be compelling to you. If more than one theory survives the exercise, ask yourself which theory has greater explanatory power, generalizability, or scope.

The theory with the greater explanatory power, generalizability, or scope probably is the better theory. If you cannot make a choice between two or more compelling theories, then you might consider theory integration. Determine whether the integrated theory is more compelling than any of the theories that were combined taken by itself.

Finally, if you believe that human beings are both determined and determining and that society is characterized fundamentally by conflict rather than by consensus, then you probably find critical theories more compelling. If this is the case, then ask yourself which model of society (the conflict model or the radical model) is the more accurate one. Consider theory integration. Decide what contributions, if any, from left realism, peacemaking criminology, feminist criminology, and post-modernism would enhance your theory. Ponder the question of whether classical/neoclassical, positivist, and critical theories can be successfully integrated.

By engaging in these exercises, you may be able to draw some informed conclusions about the causes of crime and delinquency. Remember, however, that theories must be evaluated in relation to other theories. As noted in the first chapter, theories are more or less compelling, convincing, or believable *in relation to other theories*. It is not correct to say that theories are good or bad or right or wrong, in and of themselves.

STUDY QUESTIONS

1. Why have integrated theories been produced?

2. What are some different types of integrated theory?

3. What are some of the policy implications of integrated theories?

4. What are problems with integrated theories?

5. How do integrated theories compare with theories described in previous chapters?

6. What may prove a useful method for evaluating theories?

NOTES

1. See Babbie (1992:97).

2. Tittle (1995:1). Tittle's book is about deviance, which includes crime and delinquency.

3. Of course, if a single factor, such as low IQ, lack of self-control, or economic inequality, causes crime and that factor is present at birth or

acquired early in life and remains with a person throughout his or her life, then theoretical integration is unnecessary. Such single-factor theories are sometimes referred to as "latent trait theories" in which opportunity is generally the key to whether or not a person actually commits crime. See Gottfredson and Hirschi (1990).

4. Elliott et al. (1985). Also see Elliott et al. (1979, 1989) and Wolfgang and Ferracuti (1982) for other examples of this type of theory.

5. See, for example, Lombroso (1968); Goring (1913); Glueck and Glueck (1930, 1934, 1950, 1967); Merton (1938); Cohen (1955); Cloward and Ohlin (1960); Maslow (1970); Halleck (1967); Wilson and Hernnstein (1985); Hirschi and Gottfredson (1987, 1989); Gottfredson and Hirschi (1990); Tittle (1995); and Akers (1998).

6. Henry and Milovanovic (1996).

7. Sampson and Laub (1992, 1993); other examples are Thornberry (1987); Patterson et al. (1989); and McCord (1991).

8. Examples include Colvin and Pauly (1983); Pearson and Weiner (1985); Vold and Bernard (1986); Groves and Sampson (1987); Braithwaite (1989); Hagan (1989); and Messner and Rosenfeld (1994).

9. Vila (1994).

10. Barak (1998).

11. Barak (1998:231–232).

12. Barak (1998:212).

13. See Barak (1998:Chap. 9); Einstadter and Henry (1995:301–310); Tittle (1995:89–123);

Gibbons (1994); Bohm (1987); Hirschi (1979); Kornhauser (1978:46–50).

14. See Tittle (1995:90).

15. Tittle (1995:93).

16. See Bernard and Snipes (1996:338).

17. See Bernard and Snipes (1996:343).

18. See Hirschi (1979); Tittle (1995).

19. On this point, Barak (1998:212) argues that "in all likelihood, criminologists will never be able to definitely ascertain the correct ordering of all the complex variables and how, over time, these influence each other." However, rather than abandon efforts at integration, Barak calls for a different type of integration, which, as noted previously, he calls a "post-postmodern synthesis."

20. Costello (1997:424); also see Hirschi (1979).

21. See Hirschi (1979). This is especially true of integrations that attempt to bridge different paradigms (for example, integrating anomie and radical theories).

22. It is important to emphasize that this is more than a counting exercise. Just because one theory has been criticized more than another theory, it does not necessarily follow that the theory with the fewest criticisms is the better theory. Not all criticisms are equally condemning; some criticisms are more telling than others. Some theories may be criticized more than other theories simply because they have commanded more interest than other theories.

References

Abrahamsen, David. 1944. *Crime and the Human Mind*. New York: Columbia University Press.

_____. 1960. *The Psychology of Crime*. New York: Columbia University Press.

Agnew, Robert. 1985a. "Social Control Theory and Delinquency: A Longitudinal Test." *Criminology* 23:47–61.

_____. 1985b. "A Revised Strain Theory of Delinquency." *Social Forces* 64:151–167.

_____. 1992. "Foundation for a General Strain Theory of Crime and Delinquency." *Criminology* 30:47–87.

Aichorn, August. 1935. *Wayward Youth*. New York: Viking.

Akers, Ronald L. 1967. "Problems in the Sociology of Deviance: Social Definitions and Behavior." *Social Forces* 46:455–465.

_____. 1985. *Deviant Behavior: A Social Learning Approach*. 3d ed. Belmont, CA: Wadsworth.

_____. 1994. *Criminological Theories: Introduction and Evaluation*. Los Angeles, CA: Roxbury.

_____. 1998. *Social Learning and Social Structure: A General Theory of Crime and Deviance*. Boston: Northeastern University Press.

_____. 1999. "Social Learning and Social Structure: Reply to Sampson, Morash, and Krohn." *Theoretical Criminology* 3:477–493.

Alexander, Franz and William Healy. 1935. *Roots of Crime*. New York: Knopf.

Andrews, D. A. 1980. "Some Experimental Investigations of the Principles of Differential Association Through Deliberate Manipulations of the Structure of Service

Systems." *American Sociological Review* 45:448–462.

———— and James Bonta. 1994. *The Psychology of Criminal Conduct*. Cincinnati, OH: Anderson.

Arrigo, Bruce and T. R. Young. 1997. "Chaos, Complexity, and Crime: Working Tools for a Postmodern Criminology." Pp. 77–84 in B. D. MacLean and D. Milovanovic (eds.), *Thinking Critically About Crime*. Vancouver, BC: Collective Press.

Babbie, Earl. 1992. *The Practice of Social Research*. 6th ed. Belmont, CA: Wadsworth.

Balkan, Sheila, Ronald J. Berger, and Janet Schmidt. 1980. *Crime and Deviance in America: A Critical Approach*. Belmont, CA: Wadsworth.

Bandura, Albert and Richard H. Walters. 1963. *Social Learning and Personality Development*. New York: Holt, Rinehart and Winston.

Barak, Gregg. 1988. "Newsmaking Criminology: Reflections on the Media, Intellectuals, and Crime." *Justice Quarterly* 5:565–587.

———— (ed.). 1994. *Media, Process and the Social Construction of Crime: Studies in Newsmaking Criminology*. New York: Garland.

————. 1998. *Integrating Criminologies*. Boston: Allyn and Bacon.

————, Stuart Henry, and Dragan Milovanovic. 1997. "Constitutive Criminology: An Overview of an Emerging Postmodernist School." Pp. 93–99 in B. D. MacLean and D. Milovanovic (eds.), *Thinking Critically About Crime*. Vancouver, BC: Collective Press.

Beccaria, Cesare. 1975. *On Crimes and Punishments*. Tr., with introduction,

by Harry Paolucci. Indianapolis, IN: Bobbs-Merrill.

Becker, Carl L. 1932. *The Heavenly City of the Eighteenth Century Philosophers*. New Haven, CT: Yale University Press.

Becker, Howard S. 1963. *Outsiders: Studies in the Sociology of Deviance*. New York: Free Press of Glencoe.

Beckett, Katherine. 1997. *Making Crime Pay: Law and Order in Contemporary American Politics*. New York: Oxford University Press.

Bedau, Hugo Adam. 1982. *The Death Penalty in America*. 3d ed. New York: Oxford University Press.

Beirne, Piers. 1991. "Inventing Criminology: The 'Science of Man' in Cesare Beccaria's Dei Delitti E Delle Pene (1764)." *Criminology* 29:777–820.

———— and James Messerschmidt. 2000. *Criminology*. 3d ed. Boulder, CO: Westview Press.

Bernard, Thomas J. and Jeffrey B. Snipes. 1996. "Theoretical Integration in Criminology." Pp. 301–348 in Michael Tonry (ed.), *Crime and Justice: A Review of Research* (Vol. 20). Chicago: University of Chicago Press.

Berofsky, Bernard. 1973. "Free Will and Determinism." Pp. 236–242 in P. P. Wiener (ed.), *Dictionary of the History of Ideas: Studies of Selected Pivotal Ideas* (Vol. II). New York: Charles Scribner's Sons.

Blumer, Herbert. 1969. *Symbolic Interactionism*. Englewood Cliffs, NJ: Prentice-Hall.

Bohm, Robert M. 1981. "Reflexivity and Critical Criminology." Pp. 29–47 in Gary F. Jensen (ed.),

Sociology of Delinquency: Current Issues. Beverly Hills, CA: Sage.

———. 1982. "Radical Criminology: An Explication." *Criminology* 19:565–589.

———. 1987. "Comment on 'Traditional Contributions to Radical Criminology' by Groves and Sampson." *Journal of Research in Crime and Delinquency* 24:324–331.

———. 1999. *Deathquest: An Introduction to the Theory and Practice of Capital Punishment in the United States.* Cincinnati, OH: Anderson.

——— and Keith N. Haley. 1999. *Introduction to Criminal Justice.* 2d ed. New York: Glencoe/McGraw-Hill.

Bonger, Willem. 1916. *Criminology and Economic Conditions.* Boston: Little, Brown.

Braithwaite, John. 1989. *Crime, Shame and Reintegration.* Cambridge: Cambridge University Press.

Brantingham, Paul J. and Patricia L. Brantingham. 1984. *Patterns of Crime.* New York: Macmillan.

———. 1991. *Environmental Criminology.* Prospect Heights, IL: Waveland.

Brennan, Joseph Gerard. 1953. *The Meaning of Philosophy.* 2d ed. New York: Harper & Row.

Bromberg, Walter and Charles B. Thompson. 1937. "The Relation of Psychosis, Mental Defect, and Personality Types to Crime." *Journal of Criminal Law and Criminology* 28:70–89.

Burgess, Robert L. and Ronald L. Akers. 1966. "A Differential Association-Reinforcement Theory of Criminal Behavior." *Social Problems* 14:128–147.

Bursik, Robert. 1984. "Urban Dynamics and Ecological Studies of Delinquency." *Social Forces* 63:393–413.

Cahn, Lenore (ed.). 1966. *Confronting Injustice.* Boston: Little, Brown.

Chambliss, William J. 1976. "Functional and Conflict Theories of Crime: The Heritage of Emile Durkheim and Karl Marx." Pp. 1–28 in W. J. Chambliss and M. Mankoff (eds.), *Whose Law What Order?* New York: Wiley.

——— and Robert B. Seidman. 1971. *Law, Order, and Power.* Reading, MA: Addison-Wesley.

Chamlin, Mitchell and John Cochran. 1997. "Social Altruism and Crime." *Criminology* 35:203–227.

Chesney-Lind, Meda and Barbara Bloom. 1997. "Feminist Criminology: Thinking About Women and Crime." Pp. 45–55 in B. D. MacLean and D. Milovanovic (eds.), *Thinking Critically About Crime.* Vancouver, BC: Collective Press.

Chisholm, Roderick M. 1966. *Theory of Knowledge.* Englewood Cliffs, NJ: Prentice-Hall.

Chomsky, Noam. 1969. *American Power and the New Mandarins: Historical and Political Essays.* New York: Vintage Books.

Christian, James L. 1977. *Philosophy.* 2d ed. New York: Holt, Reinhart and Winston.

Cisneros, Henry G. 1995. *Defensible Space: Deterring Crime and Building Community.* Rockville, MD: U.S. Department of Housing and Urban Development.

Cleckley, Hervey. 1982. *The Mask of Sanity.* 4th ed. St. Louis, MO: Mosby.

Cloward, Richard A. and Lloyd E. Ohlin. 1960. *Delinquency and Opportunity: A Theory of Delinquent Gangs*. New York: Free Press.

Cohen, Albert K. 1955. *Delinquent Boys: The Culture of the Gang*. New York: Free Press.

Cohen, Lawrence E. and Marcus Felson. 1979. "Social Change and Crime Rate Trends: A Routine Activity Approach." *American Sociological Review* 44:588–608.

Colvin, Mark and John Pauly. 1983. "A Critique of Criminology: Toward an Integrated Structural-Marxist Theory of Delinquency Production." *American Journal of Sociology* 89:513–551.

Comte, Auguste. 1974. *The Positive Philosophy*. New York: AMS Press.

Cooley, Charles H. 1964. *Human Nature and the Social Order*. New York: Schocken.

Cornish, Derek and Ronald Clarke (eds.). 1986. *The Reasoning Criminal: Rational Choice Perspectives on Offending*. New York: Springer-Verlag.

Cortes, Juan B. with Florence M. Gatti. 1972. *Delinquency and Crime: A Biopsychological Approach*. New York: Seminar Press.

Costello, Barbara. 1997. "On the Logical Adequacy of Cultural Deviance Theories." *Theoretical Criminology* 1:403–428.

Cullen, Francis T. 1994. "Social Support as an Organizing Concept for Criminology: Presidential Address to the Academy of Criminal Justice Sciences." *Justice Quarterly* 11:527–559.

_____, Paul Gendreau, G. Roger Jarjoura, and John Paul Wright. 1997. "Crime and the Bell Curve: Lessons from Intelligent Science." *Crime & Delinquency* 43:387–411.

_____ and John Paul Wright. 1997. "Liberating the Anomie-Strain Paradigms: Implications from Social-Support Theory." Pp. 187–206 in Nikos Passas and Robert Agnew (eds.), *The Future of Anomie Theory*. Boston: Northeastern University Press.

Curran, Daniel J. and Claire M. Renzetti. 1994. *Theories of Crime*. Boston: Allyn and Bacon.

Currie, Elliott. 1997a. "Market, Crime and Community: Toward a Mid-Range Theory of Post-Industrial Violence." *Theoretical Criminology* 1:147–172.

_____. 1997b. "Market Society and Social Disorder." Pp. 37–42 in B. D. MacLean and D. Milovanovic (eds.), *Thinking Critically About Crime*. Vancouver, BC: Collective Press.

Dahrendorf, Ralf. 1959. *Class and Class Conflict in Industrial Society*. Stanford, CA: Stanford University Press.

Dalgard, Odd S. and Einar Kringlen. 1976. "A Norwegian Twin Study of Criminology." *British Journal of Criminology* 16:213–232.

Daly, Kathleen and Meda Chesney-Lind. 1988. "Feminism and Criminology." *Justice Quarterly* 5:497–538.

Daly, Kathleen and Lisa Maher (eds.). 1998. *Criminology at the Crossroads: Feminist Readings in Crime and Justice*. New York: Oxford University Press.

Davis, Kingsley. 1971. "Prostitution." In Robert K. Merton and Robert Nisbit (eds.), *Contemporary Social Problems*. New York: Harcourt Brace Jovanovich.

Davis, Nanette J. 1975. *Sociological Constructions of Deviance: Perspectives and Issues in the Field.* Dubuque, IA: Wm. C. Brown.

DeFronzo, James. 1997. "Welfare and Homicide." *Journal of Research in Crime and Delinquency* 34:395–406.

Denno, Deborah. 1985. "Sociological and Human Developmental Explanations of Crime: Conflict or Consensus." *Criminology* 23:711–741.

Dowie, Mark. 1977. "Pinto Madness." *Mother Jones* 2:18–22.

Dubin, Robert. 1959. "Deviant Behavior and Social Structure: Continuities in Social Theory." *American Sociological Review* 24:147–164.

Dugdale, Richard L. 1877. *The Jukes: A Study in Crime, Pauperism, Disease and Heredity.* New York: Putnam.

Durkheim, Emile. 1933. *The Division of Labor in Society.* Tr. by George Simpson. New York: Free Press.

———. 1964. *The Rules of Sociological Method.* Tr. by Sarah A. Solovay and John H. Mueller; Ed. by George E. G. Catlin. New York: Free Press.

Einstadter, Werner and Stuart Henry. 1995. *Criminological Theory: An Analysis of Its Underlying Assumptions.* Fort Worth, TX: Harcourt Brace.

Elliot, Delbert S., Suzanne S. Ageton, and Rachelle J. Cantor. 1979. "An Integrated Theoretical Perspective on Delinquent Behavior." *Journal of Research in Crime and Delinquency* 16:3–27.

Elliot, Delbert S., David Huizinga, and Suzanne S. Ageton. 1985. *Explaining Delinquency and Drug Use.* Beverly Hills, CA: Sage.

———. 1989. *Multiple Problem Youth: Delinquency, Substance Abuse, and Mental Health Problems.* New York: Springer-Verlag.

Ellis, Lee and Anthony Walsh. 1997. "Gene-Based Evolutionary Theories in Criminology." *Criminology* 35:229–276.

Estabrook, Arthur H. 1916. *The Jukes in 1915.* Washington, DC: Carnegie Institute of Washington.

Eyre, Kathy. 1988. "Hearing Disorders Contribute to Criminal Behavior." *The Anniston (AL) Star* (September 11), p. 13A.

Ferrell, Jeff. 1993. *Crimes of Style: Urban Graffiti and the Politics of Criminality.* New York: Garland.

———. 1997. "Against the Law: Anarchist Criminology." Pp. 146–154 in B. D. MacLean and D. Milovanovic (eds.), *Thinking Critically About Crime.* Vancouver, BC: Collective Press.

———. 1999. "Anarchist Criminology and Social Justice." Pp. 93–108 in Bruce A. Arrigo (ed.), *Social Justice/Criminal Justice: The Maturation of Critical Theory in Law, Crime, and Deviance.* Belmont, CA: West/Wadsworth.

Finckenauer, James O. 1982. *Scared Straight! and the Panacea Phenomenon.* Englewood Cliffs, NJ: Prentice-Hall.

Fishbein, Diana H. 1990. "Biological Perspectives in Criminology." *Criminology* 28:27–72.

———. 2000. *The Science, Treatment, and Prevention of Antisocial Behaviors: Application to the Criminal Justice System.* Kingston, NJ: Civic Research Institute.

——— and Robert Thatcher. 1986. "New Diagnostic Methods in Criminology: Assessing Organic

Sources of Behavioral Disorders." *Journal of Research in Crime and Delinquency* 23:240–267.

"Footnotes." 1987. *The Chronicle of Higher Education* (October 21), p. A6.

Foucault, Michel. 1977. *Discipline and Punish: The Birth of the Prison.* New York: Pantheon Books.

Freud, Sigmund. 1953. *A General Introduction to Psychoanalysis.* New York: Permabooks.

Friedlander, Kate. 1947. *The Psychoanalytical Approach to Juvenile Delinquency.* London: International Universities Press.

Friedrichs, David O. 1996. *Trusted Criminals: White Collar Crime in Contemporary Society.* Belmont, CA: Wadsworth.

Gibbons, Don C. 1994. *Talking About Crime and Criminals: Problems and Issues in Theory Development in Criminology.* Englewood Cliffs, NJ: Prentice-Hall.

Glaser, Daniel. 1956. "Criminality Theories and Behavioral Images." *American Journal of Sociology* 61:433–444.

Glueck, Shelden. 1956. "Theory and Fact in Criminology: A Criticism of Differential Association." *British Journal of Delinquency* 7:92–109.

Glueck, Shelden and Eleanor Glueck. 1930. *500 Criminal Careers.* New York: Knopf.

_____. 1934. *One Thousand Juvenile Delinquents.* Cambridge: Harvard University Press.

_____. 1950. *Unraveling Juvenile Delinquency.* Cambridge: Harvard University Press.

_____. 1956. *Physique and Delinquency.* New York: Harper.

_____. 1967. *Predicting Delinquency and Crime.* Cambridge: Harvard University Press.

Goddard, Henry H. 1914. *Feeblemindedness: Its Causes and Consequences.* New York: Macmillan.

Gordon, David M. 1976. "Class and the Economics of Crime." Pp. 193–214 in W. J. Chambliss and M. Mankoff (eds.), *Whose Law What Order?* New York: Wiley.

Gordon, Robert. 1976. "Prevalence: The Rare Datum in Delinquency Measurement and Its Implications for the Theory of Delinquency." Pp. 201–284 in Malcolm W. Klein (ed.), *The Juvenile Justice System.* Beverly Hills, CA: Sage.

Goring, Charles. 1913. *The English Convict: A Statistical Study.* London: HMSO (reprinted by Patterson Smith, Montclair, NJ, 1972).

Gottfredson, Michael R. and Travis Hirschi. 1990. *A General Theory of Crime.* Stanford, CA: Stanford University Press.

Gould, Stephen Jay. 1981. *The Mismeasure of Man.* New York: Norton.

Gouldner, Alvin W. 1971. *The Coming Crisis of Western Sociology.* New York: Avon.

_____. 1976. *The Dialectic of Ideology and Technology: The Origins, Grammar, and Future of Ideology.* New York: Seabury Press.

Gove, Walter. 1985. "The Effect of Age and Gender on Deviant Behavior: A Biopsychological Perspective." Pp. 115–144 in A. S. Rossi (ed.), *Gender and the Life Course.* New York: Aldine.

Groves, W. Byron and Robert J. Sampson. 1987. "Traditional Contributions to Radical Criminology." *Journal of Research in Crime and Delinquency* 24:181–214.

Hagan, John. 1989. *Structural Criminology*. New Brunswick, NJ: Rutgers University Press.

Hall, Calvin S. 1954. *A Primer of Freudian Psychology*. New York: World Publishing Co.

Halleck, Seymour L. 1967. *Psychiatry and the Dilemmas of Crime*. New York: Harper and Row.

Healy, William and Augusta Bonner. 1926. *Delinquents and Criminals: Their Making and Unmaking*. New York: Macmillan.

_____. 1936. *New Light on Delinquency and Its Treatment*. New Haven, CT: Yale University Press.

Henry, Stuart and Dragan Milovanovic. 1991. "Constitutive Criminology: The Maturation of Critical Theory." *Criminology* 29:293–315.

_____. 1996. *Constitutive Criminology: Beyond Postmodernism*. London: Sage.

Herrnstein, Richard J. and Charles Murray. 1994. *The Bell Curve: Intelligence and Class Structure in American Life*. New York: Free Press.

Hirschi, Travis. 1969. *Causes of Delinquency*. Berkeley, CA: University of California Press.

_____. 1979. "Separate but Unequal Is Better." *Journal of Research in Crime and Delinquency* 16:34–38.

Hirschi, Travis and Michael Gottfredson. 1987. "Causes of White-Collar Crime." *Criminology* 25:949–974.

_____. 1989. "The Significance of White-Collar Crime for a General Theory of Crime." *Criminology* 27:359–372.

Hirschi, Travis and Michael J. Hindelang. 1977. "Intelligence and Delinquency: A Revisionist Review." *American Sociological Review* 42:572–587.

Honer, Stanley and Thomas C. Hunt. 1968. *Invitation to Philosophy*. Belmont, CA: Wadsworth.

Howe, Adrian. 1997. "Criminology Meets Postmodern Feminism (and Has a Nice Day)." Pp. 85–92 in B. D. MacLean and D. Milovanovic (eds.), *Thinking Critically About Crime*. Vancouver, BC: Collective Press.

Hudson, Barbara. 1997. "Punishment or Redress: Current Themes in European Abolitionist Criminology." Pp. 131–138 in B. D. MacLean and D. Milovanovic (eds.), *Thinking Critically About Crime*. Vancouver, BC: Collective Press.

Hutchins, Robert Maynard (ed.). 1952. *The Major Works of Sigmund Freud*. Chicago: Encyclopedia Britannica.

Jacobs, James B. 1998. "Emergence and Implications of American Hate Crime Jurisprudence." Pp. 150–176 in Robert J. Kelly and Jess Maghan (eds.), *Hate Crime: The Global Politics of Polarization*. Carbondale, IL: Southern Illinois University Press.

Jeffery C. Ray. 1965. "Criminal Behavior and Learning Theory." *Journal of Criminal Law, Criminology, and Police Science* 56:294–300.

_____. 1977. *Crime Prevention Through Environmental Design*. Beverly Hills, CA: Sage.

Jensen, Arthur R. 1998. *The g Factor: The Science of Mental Ability.* Westport, CT: Praeger.

Jones, David A. 1987. *History of Criminology: A Philosophical Perspective.* New York: Greenwood.

Jurik, Nancy C. 1999. "Socialist Feminism, Criminology, and Social Justice." Pp. 31–50 in Bruce A. Arrigo (ed.), *Social Justice/ Criminal Justice: The Maturation of Critical Theory in Law, Crime, and Deviance.* Belmont, CA: West/ Wadsworth.

Katz, Jack. 1988. *Seductions of Crime: Moral and Sensual Attractions in Doing Evil.* New York: Basic Books.

Kerlinger, Fred N. 1964. *Foundations of Behavioral Research: Educational and Psychological Inquiry.* New York: Holt, Rinehart and Winston.

Kinsey, Richard, John Lea, and Jock Young. 1986. *Losing the Fight Against Crime.* London: Basil Blackwell.

Kornhauser, Ruth Rosner. 1978. *Social Sources of Delinquency: An Appraisal of Analytic Models.* Chicago: University of Chicago Press.

Krohn, Marvin D. 1999. "Social Learning Theory: The Continuing Development of a Perspective." *Theoretical Criminology* 3:462–476.

Lanier, Mark M. and Stuart Henry. 1998. *Essential Criminology.* Boulder, CO: Westview Press.

Laub, John H. and Robert J. Sampson. 1991. "The Sutherland-Glueck Debate: On the Sociology of Criminological Knowledge." *American Journal of Sociology* 96:1402–1440.

Lea, John and Jock Young. 1984. *What Is to Be Done about Law and Order?* Harmondsworth, England: Penguin.

Lemert, Edwin M. 1951. *Social Pathology: A Systematic Approach to the Theory of Sociopathic Behavior.* New York: McGraw-Hill.

Levin, Michael. 1997. *Why Race Matters: Race Differences and What They Mean.* Westport, CT: Praeger.

Lilly, J. Robert, Francis T. Cullen, and Richard A. Ball. 1989. *Criminological Theory: Context and Consequences.* Newbury Park, CA: Sage.

Link, Bruce, Howard Andrews, and Francis Cullen. 1992. "The Violent and Illegal Behavior of Mental Patients Reconsidered." *American Sociological Review* 57:275–292.

Liska, Alan E. and M. D. Reed. 1985. "Ties to Conventional Institutions and Delinquency: Estimating Reciprocal Effects." *American Sociological Review* 50:547–560.

Lombroso, Cesare. 1968. *Crime Its Causes and Remedies.* Tr. by Henry P. Horton. Montclair, NJ: Patterson Smith.

Lynch, Michael J. and W. Byron Groves. 1989. *A Primer in Radical Criminology.* 2d ed. New York: Harrow and Heston.

MacLean, Brian D. and Dragan Milovanovic (eds.). 1997. *Thinking Critically About Crime.* Vancouver, BC: Collective Press.

Mark, Vernon H. and Frank R. Ervin. 1970. *Violence and the Brain.* New York: Harper & Row.

Martin, Randy, Robert J. Mutchnick, and W. Timothy Austin. 1990.

Criminological Thought: Pioneers Past and Present. New York: Macmillan.

Marx, Karl and Frederick Engels. 1970. *The German Ideology*. New York: International.

Maslow, Abraham H. 1970. *Motivation and Personality*. 2d ed. New York: Harper & Row.

Matsueda, Ross L. 1997. "'Cultural Deviance Theory': The Remarkable Persistence of a Flawed Term." *Theoretical Criminology* 1:429–452.

Matthews, Roger and Jock Young (eds.). 1986. *Confronting Crime*. London: Sage.

Matza, David. 1964. *Delinquency and Drift*. New York: Wiley.

_____. 1969. *Becoming Deviant*. Englewood Cliffs, NJ: Prentice-Hall.

McCord, Joan. 1991. "Family Relationship, Juvenile Delinquency, and Adult Criminality." *Criminology* 29:397–417.

Mead, Hunter. 1959. *Types and Problems of Philosophy*. New York: Henry Holt.

Merton, Robert K. 1938. "Social Structure and Anomie." *American Sociological Review* 3:672–682.

Messerschmidt, James W. 1986. *Capitalism, Patriarchy, and Crime: Toward a Socialist Feminist Criminology*. Totowa, NJ: Rowman and Littlefield.

_____. 1997. "Structured Action Theory: Understanding the Interrelation of Gender, Race, Class, and Crime." Pp. 67–74 in B. D. MacLean and D. Milovanovic (eds.), *Thinking Critically About Crime*. Vancouver, BC: Collective Press.

Messner, Steven F. and Richard Rosenfeld. 1994. *Crime and the American Dream*. Belmont, CA: Wadsworth.

Michalowski, Ray. 1990. "Niggers, Welfare Scum, and Homeless Assholes: The Problems of Idealism, Consciousness, and Context in Left Realism." *The Critical Criminologist* 2:5–6, 17–18.

Miller, Walter B. 1958. "Lower Class Culture as a Generating Milieu of Gang Delinquency." *Journal of Social Issues* 14:5–19.

Mills, C. Wright. 1942. "The Professional Ideology of Social Pathologists." *American Journal of Sociology* 49:165–180.

_____. 1970. *The Power Elite*. New York: Oxford University Press.

Monahan, John and Henry J. Steadman. 1983. "Crime and Mental Disorder: An Epidemiological Approach." In Michael Tonry and Norval Morris (eds.), *Crime and Justice* (Vol. 4). Chicago: University of Chicago Press.

Montague, William Pepperell. 1953. *The Ways of Knowing*. New York: MacMillian.

Morris, Charles G. with Albert A. Maisto. 1998. *Psychology: An Introduction*. 10th ed. Upper Saddle River, NJ: Prentice-Hall.

National Institute for Juvenile Justice and Delinquency Prevention. 1977. *Preventing Delinquency* (Vol. 1). U.S. Department of Justice, Office of Juvenile Justice and Delinquency Prevention, Law Enforcement Assistance Administration. Washington, DC: U.S. Government Printing Office.

Newman, Oscar. 1976. *Defensible Space: Crime Prevention Through Urban Design*. New York: Collier.

Nye, F. Ivan. 1958. *Family Relationships and Delinquent Behavior.* New York: Wiley.

Pallone, Nathaniel and James Hennessy. 1998. "Brain Dysfunction and Criminal Violence." *Society* 35:21–27.

Park, Robert E., Ernest W. Burgess, and Roderick D. McKenzie. 1928. *The City.* Chicago: University of Chicago Press.

Paternoster, Raymond. 1987. "The Deterrent Effect of Perceived Certainty and Severity of Punishment: A Review of the Evidence and Issues." *Justice Quarterly* 4:173–217.

Patterson, G. R., Barbara DeBaryshe, and Elizabeth Ramsey. 1989. "A Developmental Perspective on Antisocial Behavior." *American Psychologist* 44:329–335.

Pearson, Frank S. and Neil Alan Weiner. 1985. "Toward an Integration of Criminological Theories." *Journal of Criminal Law and Criminology* 76:116–150.

Pepinsky, Hal. 1999. "Peacemaking Primer." Pp. 52–70 in Bruce A. Arrigo (ed.), *Social Justice/Criminal Justice: The Maturation of Critical Theory in Law, Crime, and Deviance.* Belmont, CA: West/Wadsworth.

Pepinsky, Harold E. and Richard Quinney (eds.). 1991. *Criminology as Peacemaking.* Bloomington, IN: Indiana University Press.

_____. 1997. "Thinking Critically About Peacemaking: Reflections from Two Proponents." Pp. 109–117 in B. D. MacLean and D. Milovanovic (eds.), *Thinking Critically About Crime.* Vancouver, BC: Collective Press.

Pfohl, Stephen and Avery Gordon. 1986. "Criminological Displacements: A Sociological Deconstruction." *Social Problems* 33:94–113.

Platt, Tony. 1975. "Prospects for a Radical Criminology in the USA." Pp. 95–112 in I. Taylor et al. (eds.), *Critical Criminology.* Boston: Routledge & Kegan Paul.

Quinney, Richard. 1970. *The Social Reality of Crime.* Boston: Little, Brown.

_____. 1974. *Critique of Legal Order: Crime Control in Capitalist Society.* Boston: Little, Brown.

_____. 1977. *Class, State and Crime.* New York: McKay.

Rachlin, Howard. 1976. *Introduction to Modern Behaviorism.* 2d ed. San Francisco: W.H. Freeman.

Rafter, Nicole Hahn. 1997. "Psychopathy and the Evolution of Criminological Knowledge." *Theoretical Criminology* 1:235–259.

Raine, Adrian, Monte Buchsbaum, and Lori LaCasse. 1997. "Brain Abnormalities in Murderers Indicated by Positron Emission Tomography." *Biological Psychiatry* 42:495–508.

Reckless, Walter C. 1961. "A New Theory of Delinquency and Crime." *Federal Probation* 25:42–46.

Redl, Fritz and David Wineman. 1951. *Children Who Hate.* New York: Free Press.

_____. 1952. *Controls from Within.* New York: Free Press.

Reiss, Albert J. 1951. "Delinquency as the Failure of Personal and Social Controls." *American Sociological Review* 16:196–207.

Ritzer, George. 1975. *Sociology: A Multiple Paradigm Science.* Boston: Allyn and Bacon.

Robinson, Matthew B. 1999. "The Theoretical Development of Crime Prevention Through Environmental Design (CPTED)." Pp. 427–462 in William Laufer and Freda Adler (eds.), *Advances in Criminological Theory* (Vol. 8). New Brunswick, NJ: Transaction.

Rosner, Richard. 1979. "Adolescents Accused of Murder and Manslaughter: A Five-Year Descriptive Study." *Bulletin of the American Academy of Psychiatry and the Law* 7:342–351.

Runes, Dagobert D. (ed.). 1968. *Dictionary of Philosophy*. Totowa, NJ: Littlefield, Adams.

Rushton, J. Philippe. 1995. *Race, Evolution, and Behavior: A Life History Perspective*. New Brunswick, NJ: Transaction.

Ryan, William. 1976. *Blaming the Victim*. New York: Vintage.

Saint-Simon, Henri De. 1964. *Social Organization, the Science of Man and Other Writings*. Ed. & Tr. by Felix Markham. New York: Harper Torchbooks.

Salopek, Paul. 1997. "What's Next for Mankind?" *The Orlando Sentinel* (from the *Chicago Tribune*) (June 1), p. G-1.

Sampson, Robert J. 1999. "Techniques of Research Neutralization." *Theoretical Criminology* 3:438–451.

_____ and W. Byron Groves. 1989. "Community Structure and Crime: Testing Social Disorganization Theory." *American Journal of Sociology* 94:774–802.

Sampson, Robert J. and John H. Laub. 1992. "Crime and Deviance in the Life Course." *Annual Review of Sociology* 24:509–525.

_____. 1993. *Crime in the Making: Pathways and Turning Points Through Life*. Cambridge: Harvard University Press.

Schlossman, Steven, Gail Zellman, and Richard Shavelson, with Michael Sedlak and Jane Cobb. 1984. *Delinquency Prevention in South Chicago: A Fifty-Year Assessment of the Chicago Area Project*. Santa Monica, CA: Rand.

Schuessler, Karl F. and Donald R. Cressey. 1950. "Personality Characteristics of Criminals." *American Journal of Sociology* 55:476–484.

Schur, Edwin M. 1969. *Our Criminal Society*. Englewood Cliffs, NJ: Prentice-Hall.

_____. 1973. *Radical Nonintervention*. Englewood Cliffs, NJ: Prentice-Hall.

Schwartz, Martin D. 1989. "The Undercutting Edge of Criminology." *The Critical Criminologist* 1:1, 2, 5.

Schwartz, Martin and Walter DeKeseredy. 1991. "Left Realist Criminology: Strengths, Weaknesses and the Feminist Critique." *Crime, Law and Social Change* 15:51–72.

Schwendinger, Herman and Julia Schwendinger. 1975, originally 1970. "Defenders of Order or Guardians of Human Rights?" Pp. 113–146 in I. Taylor et al. (eds.), *Critical Criminology*. Boston: Routledge & Kegan Paul.

_____. 1983. *Rape and Inequality*. Beverly Hills, CA: Sage.

Sellin, Thorstein. 1938. *Culture, Conflict and Crime*. New York: Social Science Research Council.

Shah, Saleem and Loren H. Roth. 1974. "Biological and Psycho-physiological Factors in Criminality." Pp. 101–173 in Daniel Glaser (ed.), *Handbook of Criminology*. Chicago: Rand.

Shaw, Clifford R. 1929. *Delinquency Areas*. Chicago: University of Chicago Press.

_____. 1930. *The Jackroller*. Chicago: University of Chicago Press.

_____. 1931. *The Natural History of a Delinquent Career*. Chicago: University of Chicago Press.

_____. 1938. *Brothers in Crime*. Chicago: University of Chicago Press.

Shaw, Clifford R. and Henry D. McKay. 1931. *Social Factors in Juvenile Delinquency*. Chicago: University of Chicago Press.

_____. 1942. *Juvenile Delinquency and Urban Areas*. Chicago: University of Chicago Press.

Sheldon, William H. 1949. *Varieties of Delinquent Youth*. New York: Harper.

Simon, David R. 1996. *Elite Deviance*. 5th ed. Boston: Allyn and Bacon.

Simon, Rita. 1975. *Women and Crime*. Lexington, MA: D.C. Heath.

Simpson, Sally S. 1989. "Feminist Theory, Crime, and Justice." *Criminology* 27:605–631.

Skogan, Wesley G. 1990. *Disorder and Decline: Crime and the Spiral of Decay in American Neighborhoods*. New York: Free Press.

Stanko, Elizabeth. 1985. *Intimate Intrusions: Women's Experience of Male Violence*. Boston: Routledge & Kegan Paul.

Stark, Rodney. 1987. "Deviant Places: A Theory of the Ecology of Crime." *Criminology* 25:893–909.

Stephens, Gene. 1987. "Crime and Punishment: Forces Shaping the Future." *The Futurist* (January-February): 18–26.

Steury, Ellen Hochstedler. 1993. "Criminal Defendants with Psychiatric Impairment: Prevalence, Probabilities and Rates." *Journal of Criminal Law and Criminology* 84:354–374.

Sullivan, Dennis. 1980. *The Mask of Love: Corrections in America, Toward a Mutual Aid Alternative*. Port Washington, NY: Kennikat Press.

Sutherland, Edwin H. and Donald R. Cressey. 1974. *Criminology*. 9th ed. Philadelphia: J. B. Lippincott. Reprinted by permission of the Estate of R. Cressey.

Suttles, Gerald D. 1968. *The Social Order of the Slum: Ethnicity and Territory in the Inner City*. Chicago: University of Chicago Press.

Sykes, Gresham and David Matza. 1957. "Techniques of Neutralization: A Theory of Delinquency." *American Sociological Review* 22:664–670.

Tappan, Paul W. (ed.). 1951. *Contemporary Correction*. New York: McGraw-Hill.

Tarde, Gabriel. 1968. *Penal Philosophy*. Tr. by Rapelje Howell. Montclair, NJ: Patterson Smith.

Taylor, Ian, Paul Walton, and Jock Young. 1974. *The New Criminology: For a Social Theory of Deviance*. New York: Harper & Row.

_____. 1975. *Critical Criminology*. Boston: Routledge & Kegan Paul.

Thompson, E. P. 1975. *Whigs and Hunters: The Origin of the Black Act*. New York: Pantheon.

Thornberry, Terence P. 1987. "Towards an Interactional Theory of Delinquency." *Criminology* 25:863–891.

Tittle, Charles R. 1995. *Control Balance: Toward a General Theory of Deviance*. Boulder, CO: Westview Press.

Toby, Jackson. 1957. "Social Disorganization and Stake in Conformity: Complementary Factors in the Predatory Behavior of Hoodlums." *Journal of Criminal Law, Criminology and Police Science* 48:12–17.

Turk, Austin. 1969. *Criminality and Legal Order*. Chicago: Rand.

_____. 1979. "Analyzing Official Deviance: For Nonpartisan Conflict Analyses in Criminology." *Criminology* 4:459–476.

Unger, Roberto Mangabeira. 1987. *False Necessity*. New York: Cambridge University Press.

Vila, Bryan. 1994. "A General Paradigm for Understanding Criminal Behavior: Extending Evolutionary Ecological Theory." *Criminology* 32:311–359.

_____ and Cynthia Morris (eds.). 1997. *Capital Punishment in the United States: A Documentary History*. Westport, CT: Greenwood.

Vold, George B. 1958. *Theoretical Criminology*. New York: Oxford.

_____. 1979. *Theoretical Criminology*. 2d ed. New York: Oxford.

_____ and Thomas J. Bernard. 1986. *Theoretical Criminology*. 3d ed. New York: Oxford.

Waldo, Gordon P. and Simon Dinitz. 1967. "Personality Attributes of the Criminal: An Analysis of Research Studies, 1950–1965." *Journal of Research in Crime and Delinquency* 4:185–202.

Walsh, Anthony and Lee Ellis. 1999. "Political Ideology and American Criminologists' Explanations for Criminal Behavior." *The Criminologist* 24 (No. 6, November/December):1, 14, 26–27.

Walters, Glenn. 1992. "A Meta-Analysis of the Gene-Crime Relationship." *Criminology* 30:595–613.

_____ and Thomas White. 1989. "Heredity and Crime: Bad Genes or Bad Research." *Criminology* 27:455–486.

Williams, Frank P. III and Marilyn D. McShane. 1994. *Criminological Theory*. 2d ed. Englewood Cliffs, NJ: Prentice-Hall.

Wilson, James Q. and Richard J. Herrnstein. 1985. *Crime and Human Nature*. New York: Simon and Schuster.

Wilson, William Julius. 1987. *The Truly Disadvantaged*. Chicago: University of Chicago Press.

Wolfgang, Marvin E. and Franco Ferracuti. 1982. *The Subculture of Violence*. Beverly Hills, CA: Sage.

Wood, Peter B., Walter R. Gove, James A. Wilson, and John K. Cochran. 1997. "Nonsocial Reinforcement and Habitual Criminal Conduct: An Extension of Learning Theory." *Criminology* 35:335–366.

Woodworth, Robert S. and Mary R. Sheehan. 1964. *Contemporary Schools of Psychology*. 3d ed. New York: Ronald Press.

Wright, Erik Olin. 1978. *Class, Crisis and the State*. New York: NLB.

Yochelson, Samuel and Stanton E. Samenow. 1976. *The Criminal Personality* (Vol. 1: *A Profile for Change*). Northvale, NJ: Jason Aronson.

Young, Jock. 1997. "Left Realism: The Basics." Pp. 28–36 in B.D. MacLean and D. Milovanovic (eds.), *Thinking Critically About Crime.* Vancouver, BC: Collective Press.

Zeitlin, Irving M. 1968. *Ideology and the Development of Sociological Theory.* Englewood Cliffs, NJ: Prentice-Hall.

Zinn, Howard. 1990. *A People's History of the United States.* New York: Harper Perennial.

Name Index

Subject Index